# God's People Now!

# God's People Now!

*Face to Face with
Mennonite Church
Canada*

*Robert J. Suderman*

**Herald Press**
Waterloo, Ontario
Scottdale, Pennsylvania

Library and Archives Canada Cataloguing in Publication

Suderman, Robert J.
God's people now! : face to face with Mennonite Church
Canada / Robert J. Suderman.

ISBN 978-0-8361-9378-7

1. Mennonites—Canada. 2. Mennonite Church Canada. I. Title.
BX8121.3.S94 2007 289.7'71 C2007-901688-X

GOD'S PEOPLE NOW!
Copyright © 2007 by Herald Press, Scottdale, Pa. 15683
    Published simultaneously in Canada by Herald Press,
    Waterloo, Ont. N2L 6H7. All rights reserved
Library of Congress Catalogue Card Number: 2007924177
Canadiana Entry Number: C2007-901688-X
International Standard Book Number: 978-0-8361-9378-7
Printed in the United States of America
Book design by Sandra Johnson
Cover by Ingrid Hess

12 11 10 09 08 07    10 9 8 7 6 5 4 3 2 1

To order or request information, please call 1-800-245-7894, or visit
www.heraldpress.com.

*To all who participated in and made possible
the God's People Now! listening tour.
You have served the church well.*

# Contents

# Foreword

Jack Suderman's trek across Canada, during which he visited members of every congregation in Mennonite Church Canada, is in the spirit of Paul the apostle:

> After some days Paul said to Barnabas, "Come, let us return and visit the believers in every city where we proclaimed the word of the Lord and see how they are doing.—Acts 15:36

Suderman did not plant the churches in Canada, as Paul did the congregations he visited. But both Paul and the general secretary of Mennonite Church Canada have given their lives as missionaries. Both understand the joy and challenge of living out the gospel in a multicultural world, and both take a long-term view of what God is doing with the church.

As is true for many denominations, Mennonites in North America have been buffeted by conflict and change in the past decade. Maintaining the unity of the church while living the gospel in diverse cultural settings is work of the Spirit, and God uses leaders with big vision. Even though the Mennonite Church in North America overall has not seen numerical growth in the past decade, there is rapid change. *God's People Now!* provides a valuable freeze-frame picture of the church in motion. Mennonites in Canada now speak more than a dozen languages. The church has morphed from rural Germanic agricultural communities to multicultural, often urban congregations in which many members work in the professions. Older "cradle" Mennonites, who in their youth never met a person of another world religion, now have neighbours or work colleagues who are Muslim, Hindu, or Buddhist.

No wonder the Mennonite Church has growing pains! But Jack Suderman, like Paul, has traveled among scattered congregations with the heart of a missionary and the hope of God's reign. Jack and his traveling companions rediscovered and confirmed that God is wonderfully at work even in the clay vessel we call the church.

Many leaders across Mennonite Church Canada have befriended me, and I have witnessed close-up some of turmoil conferences and congregations have been through. It is encouraging to see afresh in this book the deep commitments that unite us as a Mennonite people (chapter 3). Jack reminds us that unity is God's gift, not something we engineer.

As a pastoral and theological educator, I pay attention to what this book reveals. I take to the seminary community questions of how we can best serve a church that has relatively few young adults or that seeks leaders who can "make the Bible come alive and become more relevant." Suderman's travel notes provide data that can help seminaries, universities, mission agencies, conferences, and other entities discern what God is calling us to be.

But this book reminds us that the church is not about institutions and programs. It is about "incarnational communities of salvation"—worshipping, witnessing, and reconciling congregations (chapter 9). *God's People Now!* moves beyond data reporting to set a direction and a vision for the future. That vision is about God's work of shaping a people—ordinary and sinful individuals like you and me whom God calls into communities of wholeness and hope.

Thank you, Jack, for listening so well to the people of God and to what the Spirit is saying. Your careful listening is a model for the rest of us. Your hope and your wisdom will encourage many, and the leadership you give strengthens the church. To God be the glory.

J. Nelson Kraybill
President, Associated Mennonite Biblical Seminary
Elkhart, Indiana

# Introduction

When I was appointed general secretary of Mennonite Church Canada, I knew what I most needed to do my job well. It was to get a firsthand, up-close look at the challenges, activities, and spirit of the life of our 230 congregations. But how could this best be accomplished? In conversations with my wife, Irene, MC Canada staff, and general board members, one idea rose to the top: I needed to find a way of visiting every single congregation in our denomination, from Vancouver Island to New Brunswick and from north to south, on their "turf." I was aware that this would be a daunting undertaking, but the time to do so seemed right. Our church was in a good situation.

As a new leader I wanted to hear what the churches were saying, to understand how they were doing, and to help them hear each other. Firsthand conversations seemed to be the best tool for this. We were not in a financial crisis. In fact, giving had been good, and it would be a pleasure to thank congregations and to encourage this generous trend. This would not need to be a fund-raising tour.

Recent delegate assemblies had been positive and the trust level was up. We could build on positive feelings and expand and deepen these conversations. We do have significant issues facing our church. We will need to develop and count on much goodwill to work at them. By listening to each congregation, we would trust each other more, and this would be healthy when we face tough issues in our midst.

And so the vision for the God's People Now! listening tour

emerged with the ambitious goal of visiting every congregation in Mennonite Church Canada in a short time. Our competent staff began to organize the logistics. Area churches were invited to participate in these visits. Our executive staff volunteered to take turns accompanying me in different regions. I'm thankful my wife also was able to accompany me on significant parts of the tour.

We hoped to meet the following goals:

1. Visit each congregation in its place of worship.
2. Gather information that would help us "take the pulse" of the church.
3. Generate a positive "buzz" from congregations knowing that their issues, joys, and concerns are being listened to and taken seriously.
4. Encourage the goodwill and closer relationships that can strengthen the church and its ministries.
5. Tangibly demonstrate cooperation and partnership among congregations, area churches, and the national church. (Mennonite Church Canada uses these terms for what would be known in other areas as congregations, area conferences, and the denomination.)

The format of the conversations was not complex. I developed four simple questions, and congregations were alerted that these would be used as the basis for our ninety-minute conversation with them. The questions were as follows:

1. How are you?
2. What are you doing?
3. What are your concerns?
4. What are your needs?

We also reserved a few minutes on the agenda to offer the perspective of the national church. We said thank you on behalf of the many ministry partners at home and around the world. We shared the purpose and identity of our church as it has been defined. And we prayed with each congregation.

The God's People Now! listening tour exceeded all my expectations. Indeed, some of the more important results were those that I had not anticipated. For example, I had not expected the tears that flowed so often and so deeply. Sometimes these were tears of appreciation and joy for the visit, sometimes tears of pain and struggle. Sometimes these were tears of relief for finally being able to share worries about the church with a person who would hear them in context of the concerns of others. And often these were my own tears and those of the people who accompanied me.

I had not anticipated the sacrifice people would make to meet with us. We arrived at congregations at odd times, and the number of persons that took time off from work, lost wages to be there, and sacrificed personal agendas to make this happen was astounding. Farmers stopped their tractors for a few hours, a carpenter closed his shop and came with sawdust on his overalls, professionals took time off from work, and shift workers juggled schedules. It seemed important to people to be there.

I had not fully anticipated that our church would speak about itself so honestly, passionately, fearfully, sorrowfully, and joyfully. Persons and leaders were willing to make themselves vulnerable in front of these "knowing strangers." And frequently we were told how helpful it had been for them to think through the simple questions we had asked.

I had not anticipated that these visits would serve as a catalyst for conversation within the congregations themselves. Often we were told that they had never talked to each other like this before and that they had not said some important things in each other's presence before. Our presence and listening ears seemed to liberate folks to speak to each other.

And I had not anticipated the growing perception that this tour was a significant act of leadership in the church. The idea was simple, but it seemed to catch the imagination of young and old as being a good, timely, and important thing to do. Many pastors told us that they would do something akin to this in their own congregation.

During the tour, I was often asked how I was doing, if I was tired, and if the experience was encouraging or overwhelming. There were times of exhaustion and periods of deep dismay and struggle. Visiting over two hundred congregations in seventy-one days and inviting people to tell their stories resulted in significant sharing of joys and deep pain, and it was an ambitious undertaking. Before I began, I fully expected to be discouraged by what I would encounter. But invariable I was more impressed, energized, and encouraged by the visits than I was discouraged. Our church is an instrument of hope, committed to its vocation of bringing God's healing to a challenging world.

Our people are wise and creative, and I eagerly wrote down the wonderful ways in which they described what it means to be the church in the twenty-first century. In my mind, the most significant parts of this book are the quotes I gleaned from our people. These are delightful, creative, salty, pointed, humorous, and sad. They made us laugh and cry. They also reveal the pain that is present among us. These quotes reflect the graciousness and generosity that characterizes our people. My desire in this book is to communicate faithfully what I heard so that the church can listen to itself. I trust that the quotes and my reflections on them can serve to inform and inspire us as we reflect on our vocation of being God's people now.

We gained remarkable insights about God's people and specifically about Mennonite Church Canada. This book is a modest way of giving back some of what we experienced and learned. God's people care deeply about the church and each other. They desire to be faithful to God, and they sincerely want to be who God wants them to be. My hope is that others may be encouraged and inspired as I was while listening to our experiences of being God's people now.

This book contains my reflections on the experience. However, I trust that the reader will understand that the heart of the book is what others have contributed. It was the wisdom of our people that inspired my passion to share what I have heard. And the quotes in this book represent but one small layer of the wisdom and insight we heard.

Some of these quotes are interspersed into the chapters in the spirit of illustrations. All are gathered in the appendix by topic. The heroes of the book are the people of our churches. It is their insight that I am trying to respect and convey. They have inspired me and provided hope for the future of the church.

I want to say a special and a deeply felt thank-you to so many who contributed to making the tour and the book a reality. To our executive and other staff who sacrificially gave of themselves to accompany this tour and who took on extra duties in my absence. To the operations team that worked persistently and with excellence at the details and logistics of the tour. To the rest of our staff, who needed to function more independently while their supervisors were away, especially to my own executive assistant, who kept things running so smoothly. To all those from the area churches who were able to participate in parts of the visits. Special mention and thanks go to David Martin, executive minister of Mennonite Church Eastern Canada, who accompanied me to all but one congregation in that region. To our general board and councils that affirmed and encouraged this process in many ways. To my wife Irene, who participated in parts of the tour and steadfastly encouraged it as a good thing, even though that meant my being away from home more often. To the editors and staff of Mennonite Publishing Network for their willingness to undertake this project. To the pastors and leaders of congregations who did not see our visit as a threat but as an opportunity for growth in their congregations. To the special editors who helped prepare the material and make it more readable. To our communications staff, who creatively provided ideas in communicating the results of the tour. And to the hundreds of persons who opened their hearts and gave their time to us, meeting us at unusual hours and pouring out their hearts to us.

This book is a very modest effort to give back what we received, so that the church can hear itself and use what is heard for the glory of God.

# 1

# Face to Face

So, what did we experience on the God's People Now! tour?

In broad strokes, we experienced that our name, Mennonite Church Canada, aptly describes who we are and what we want to become.

We are *Mennonite*. There is a fierce insistence on our Mennonite/Anabaptist identity. This identity, however, is variously understood within and among those of Swiss, Latin American, German, Asian, French, Russian, Native Canadian, and other ethnic backgrounds. Some continue to define identity in terms of particular ethnic and cultural heritages, while others passionately define Mennonite identity only in terms of faith.

We are a *church*. There is a strong desire to be the church together, beyond any particular congregational or regional expression of being church. We are serious about our vocation in the world: we are and we want to be God's people now.

And we are *Canadian*. It is clear that our church is impacted and shaped by the broader culture. We are experiencing shifts and trends that are also present in our country. We are both modern and postmodern; we mirror vestiges of Christendom, even though it is crumbling around us, and our spirituality is nurtured by pluralism, secularism,

> ## "Every time someone leaves, part of our heart goes with them."

consumerism, and materialism. Within this context we yearn to be faithful to God's Spirit.

From Black Creek, Vancouver Island (west), to Petitcodiac, New Brunswick (east); from Leamington, Ontario (south), to Cross Lake, Manitoba (north), Mennonite Church Canada is ministering to God's reign in our country. From the smallest congregation (eleven members) to the largest (over a thousand members), Mennonite Church Canada is nurturing, discipling, and encouraging its people.

"Transition will be a permanent part of life, and we need to learn to deal with transition."

"The church can't address the crisis in agriculture. But the church can address the crisis in the lives of the people."

In thirteen languages and among many cultures (there are forty-three congregations whose first language is neither German nor English) Mennonite Church Canada is proclaiming the reconciling gospel of Jesus Christ. From the oldest congregation in Canada (there is a friendly rivalry whether this is First Mennonite Church in Vineland or Rainham Mennonite Church in Selkirk, Ontario) to the newest congregations (the Gathering in Kitchener and the Laotian Canadian Mennonite Evangelical Church in Toronto), Mennonite Church Canada is embracing evangelism and growth.

Our congregations have identifiable demographic bulges (seniors) and gaps (eighteen- to twenty-eight-year-olds). We face significant challenges in rural areas (depopulation in Saskatchewan and Alberta; high costs of farming and low commodity prices) and in urban centres (inner-city poverty; multiplicity of competing options; chronic busyness of members). But within these challenges MC Canada is struggling to be faithful to God's will and way.

Our congregations are facing some divisive and conflicting practices. Preferences for worship and musical styles and responses to same-sex realities head the list. We don't always agree on how to interpret the Bible for our faith and practice. We wonder whether we should be a church with more centralized authority or if it is better to promote strong congregational autonomy. Debate on such questions is often intense and sharp. We experienced this intensity in our visits to congregations. We are a church that is hurting deeply in places but that at the same time is responding to the opportunities for ministry that are before us. There are many opportunities to engage our society, high levels of spiritual interest, and a strong desire for an authentic and faithful Christian life. MC Canada is experiencing waves of energy, joy, exuberance, and growth.

And *everywhere*, in every congregation, there is much goodwill nurtured by the golden hearts and sincerity of persons wanting to be God's faithful people. Mennonite Church Canada people are sincere, well intentioned, and eager to be effective agents of God's gospel in our world. I realized after the tour that I had not met a single person I didn't like. In spite of many difficult and heart-rending conversations, we ended each day of the tour with a profound sense of gratitude for the people in MC Canada and for what God is doing among us.

*"We've now developed an atmosphere in which folks are praying for the congregation instead of against it."*

*"Our advice is that when you come together, eat first, and then you don't have as many tensions."*

# "We always have a choice. We can choose to allow things to divide or unite us."

## Angels, Songbirds, and Seedbeds

In his book *Unmasking the Powers*, Walter Wink points out that in the book of Revelation the resurrected Jesus does not ask the writer to address the churches but rather to address "the *angel* of the church in . . . " (see Revelation 2:1, 8, 12, 18; 3:1, 7, 14). Wink suggests that every congregation is influenced, shaped, or controlled by an "angel." In order to transform congregational life, the angel that is shaping it has to be transformed or converted. Some of these angels indeed need to be converted, because they resist, overtly or subtly, the will of God. Other angels need to be fed because they encourage the congregation to greater faithfulness.

In my visits, I understood better what Wink is talking about. I encountered these angels in three very important ways:

1. All the people I met are sincere, well intentioned, and want the best, as they understand it, for the church.
2. There are "forces" at work in the lives of the congregations that prevent these good and sincere intentions from being fully realized.
3. Sometimes congregations are simply surprised by the quantity of good that comes from seemingly insignificant efforts.

Are there hints as to how these angels can be transformed or nourished? I believe one hint that emerged was the crucial importance of good leadership. Sparks of leadership can come from any part of

## "We are a seeding church; other churches are harvesting what we sow."

the congregation. It can be a "sparky" senior or an ambitious Sunday school teacher. It can be a youth or a finance chair. It can be an usher or a choir director. It can be inspirational pastoral leadership or a good council chairperson. It is often surprising where the spark comes from, but it is immediately apparent when it's there. Congregations that accept, affirm, and encourage this kind of leadership are more often seeing their "good angels" flourish and thereby shape the spirit and pulse of the congregation. Such leadership also means that "recalcitrant angels" take a back seat.

I discovered that the good, wise, and profound yet simple comments made by people often reflected the presence of these angels in their midst. Members of one small congregation told me about the daunting challenges their congregation is facing: declining population, limited success in attracting young adults into their fellowship, dwindling numbers, difficulty in meeting the expenses they had budgeted, loss of key leaders. The situation certainly appeared discouraging.

> "I'm a new Christian, and it was just the natural thing to keep coming here to church. So I prayed that if there was anything missing here I wanted to be part of supplying it."

Yet I did not sense any note of discouragement in this congregation. They clearly enjoy being with each other. They are proud that they are the church. They love each other. They support each other.

They used two special images to describe how they understand themselves. First, they described themselves as a "seed-bed church." Their special ministry seems to be to train and equip young people to love the church. When the young people leave the community for study and jobs, they take that love for the church with them. They could readily recite a long list of leaders in the church who had been nurtured in this congregation and then blessed to go out to make a contribution elsewhere. They rejoiced in the contribution and ministry of each one as if these were their own, even as the home congregation was declining. They were proud, satisfied, and fulfilled in their seedbed ministry, and they were confident that they were making a significant contribution to the church and to the world.

> *"If we don't find a solution on the first day, then we take another day, no problem. It's important to be communal."*

The second image they used is seared into my mind. An older woman, probably in her late seventies, tiny in stature but with the biggest and brightest eyes you can imagine, looked at me and said, "Our congregation is like a beautiful songbird. We are small, but we have everything we need to be who we are."

*We have everything we need to be who we are.* What a profound insight into the essential nature of being the church! The apostle Paul reminds us that that the church is often strongest in its weakness. This is not a reference to bad planning or sloppy commitment. It is a reference to the confidence we need to have to "be who we are," even in the face of apparent failure. Paul goes on to talk about how this "weakness" is based on the cross of Christ, not on the contemporary wisdom and philosophies of this world. The woman who spoke seems to have understood that reality very profoundly. If we accept "who we are" then indeed we have "everything we need."

I think her word is a prophetic word of encouragement for us as a church in Canada. We are a small group in a vast country. But we have what we need to be faithful and thus to be who we are. It is also true that we are a songbird church. Our songs are heard well beyond what our size would normally allow. And we are also a seedbed church. Our church is feeding and shaping other groups, with insight and wisdom that is prophetic and helpful.

This congregation is nurtured by the immense and often un-tapped power of its imagination. Perhaps our church's greatest area of failure is its underdeveloped capacity to imagine what can be: the failure to imagine God's power at work, the failure to imagine that Jesus' cross and resurrection actually have cosmic implications.

In subsequent chapters we will look at the challenges of re-imag-ining the church, the demographic bulges and gaps, leadership, unity and diversity, the role of the *Confession of Faith in a Mennonite Perspective*, and other common themes that are evident in the church. But a good deal of the "salt and light" in these chapters comes from the quotes I gathered from church people.

Powerful and wise insights about the church came from con-gregations such as yours. We do have what we need to be who we are. The listening tour has given us many insights. The collection of wisdom from folks in MC Canada is significant, and as you read, I pray that you will be encouraged as I have been and emerge from this exposure as hopeful as I am.

# 2

# Challenges of the Church:
# Listening to Our Experience

In this chapter I will identity and reflect on ten recurrent themes that emerged in the many conversations on the tour. I'll elaborate on some themes in subsequent chapters. But here they are gathered together, roughly in order of the frequency and/or intensity of their occurrence in our conversations. With each theme I include several quotes that give poignancy and realism to my observations and reflections. These quotes from ordinary members of our church are really the heart of these reflections.

## 1. Demographic Realities

Growth in the church—or rather the lack of it—is a major preoccupation among our members. Regular church participation is declining in a number of regions, while increasing in certain other places. Often the rate of growth or decline is linked to demographics.

First, the depopulation of rural areas, especially in the prairies, is generating significant stress and distress in the congregations located there. While the rural-urban demographic shift is beyond the control of the church, the church is experiencing the impact of these realignments. Depopulation means that attendance is declining, volunteers for congrega-

*"It's important that our church not become the flavour of the month."*

tional programs are at a premium, and revenue doesn't allow the implementation of ministry dreams that are present.

*"Our church is going from a grape to a raisin."*

These realities are dampening the enthusiasm and the spirit of optimism in some congregations. A broader demographic reality is that fewer Canadians in general—rural and urban—are committing to regular church participation as a pattern for their lives. Assumptions are shifting in how people understand regular attendance and participation. Whereas "regular" attendance at church services and functions used to mean three or four times a month, it now can mean once a month.

Finally, the aging of the Canadian population in general is reflected in our churches. The baby boomers are aging, and this impacts the numbers, energy, and vision of the church. (See chapter five on seniors in the church.)

This three-fold phenomenon of depopulation, decreased participation, and aging is putting significant pressure on the capacity of congregations to offer the quality of ministry that regular attendees are used to and that they would like.

"We may have the distinction of being the only Mennonite church in Ontario located only on gravel roads."

"We have aches and pains because we're growing. These are signs that we are alive."

## 2. Unity and Diversity

Our denomination spends a great deal of energy seeking the right balance of unity and diversity. Can we find enough common ground in our church so that the rich diversity among us can truly be life giving rather than energy sapping? This question often, though not always, focuses on our understandings of sexuality and of the role of the church in advocating for or against change in sexual values. While the specific issue of homosexuality is frequently the lightning rod, the conversation often shifts quickly to discussion about how to interpret the Bible adequately and about who has the authority to make decisions on polity and practice. (See point seven below and chapter three on unity and diversity.)

*"Sharing time in worship is a big leveller; it brings together the extremes and forces each one to deal with the other. It's a discipline that helps us listen to each other."*

*"It's best to be silent, because the divisions are so deep."*

*"I have some absolute beliefs, and I'm sorry I can't back down from them. That doesn't mean I won't talk to you."*

## "We've been silenced. And it's hard to learn to be quiet over and over."

### 3. Youth and Young Adults

In our visits, it was striking how often people expressed concern over the relatively low participation of eighteen- to twenty-eight-year-olds in congregational life. Naturally, people are asking why this is so, and they are not coming to consensus on the answers. Still, congregations are eager to enlist youth and young adults for active participation. And most want to do this out of a compelling vision of what it means to be the church and not simply out of tradition and habit.

### 4. Worship, Music, and Intergenerational Dynamics

Worship style preferences, especially around music, generate a lot of passion in congregations. I use the word *passion* intentionally to describe this phenomenon, because next to the sexuality discussion, this is where anger and exuberance, conflict and joy are most often evident in our congregations.

Some congregations have worked through their conflicts over worship styles. Their members speak passionately of worship as an uplifting, nurturing, and joyous occasion where Christ's body comes together for inspiration in unity and hope. Other congregations have not achieved such peace. Often in these settings, worship is experienced as a locus of conflict, division, anger, and dissatisfaction. Whether congregations are in conflict or at peace over worship, all agree that turning the corner to healthy worship is a difficult process.

Concerns over worship are often related to the intergenerational dynamics of congregational life. Where congregations have been able to move from conflict to harmony, it has been because the various age sectors of the congregation have begun to "stand guard" for the preferences and well-being of sectors other than their own. When this happens, there is a remarkable spirit of harmony and an absence of competition among generations.

In one congregation, for example, the worship team of young people always asks the eighty-year-old-plus women if they enjoyed the words of the new songs, if the music was too loud, and if there were enough familiar songs in the service. These women, in turn, are the most vocal supporters of the youth. When I asked, "How did you get to be so encouraging to the participation of youth?" they answered, "Some years ago we weren't like this and we've all learned our lesson."

By contrast, in congregations where each age group defends its needs, preferences, and rights, walls seem to get higher and the issues become more divisive. The drums of the youth seem so much louder, and the traditional hymns of their elders become so much more boring when each group defends its rights.

What is the key to harmony? I have been surprised to hear that it is often a spark of leadership that helps a congregation "turn the corner" to health in worship. Such leadership does not necessarily come from the pastor. Someone—a senior, a council member, a deacon, or a teenager—takes some energetic initiative toward conciliation, and it makes all the difference in the world.

"We do not tolerate the question 'what do I like in a worship service?' But rather 'what enables us to worship well?' That's the question we need to answer."

"You don't worship if you hate to go to church."

## 5. Essence and Identity

When congregations deal with questions of diversity, structure, and authority, an underlying struggle is to define the essence of who they are. We heard many congregations sorting out the differences between "non-negotiable" core values and values that are not foundational. Sometimes the concerns are related to the proper use of the *Confession of Faith* in the life of the congregation, but sometimes it has to do with historical factors that go much deeper than the *Confession*.

**"The drummer is one of our members, so we have to tolerate him."**

**"You have to decide what matters more: the people or the music."**

Some, for example, understand our identity as a "peace church" to be part of the ethnic baggage of Mennonites with Swiss and Russian heritages but not biblically central to who we need to be as a church. Others would see this as the very screen that identifies us as truly Mennonite.

Some assume that our traditional understandings of same-sex relationships are part of core identity and essence as a denomination, while others feel that this can be a matter for discernment of the local or broader church.

Some would say that the way curriculum for Sunday school is chosen, the education that pastors need to have, and the ways in which pastors are selected for the congregation are subject simply to the preferences of the local congregations. Others would prefer to see more consistency and unity of criteria in these decisions across the national church. And others are simply inconsistent, assuming that the patterns of their congregations are good and those of others are not.

**"Mennonite means the love of God in action."**

"What we feed ourselves is what we get."

"We've tried to be a 'Mennonite in brackets' kind of congregation. And that doesn't work."

"If the Anglican Book of Common Prayer was good enough for Paul and Silas, it's good enough for us."

"Twenty years ago we made the decision to stop using conference Sunday school material and started using David Cook instead. Since then we've 'won' some people, but we've lost our peoplehood."

## 6. Leadership Development

Our churches want to develop creative, energized, imaginative, and Anabaptist leadership that will help them navigate the sometimes turbulent waters of the twenty-first century. Some leaders may be highly energized but scarcely Anabaptist; others may try to be very Anabaptist but are not imaginative. Many recognize that the church will require a special breed of leadership to move forward with joy and conviction in our century.

The formal training opportunities of our denominational seminaries and colleges are touching only a small percent of our actual and potential leadership. Consequently, many of the leaders in our congregations have little or no formal leadership or theological training that is Mennonite.

Congregations are calling for better leadership training to be available locally, so that prospective leaders need not interrupt their lives with several years away at a seminary or college. If denominational training is not accessible locally, then they access training that is local, and this may or may not nurture Anabaptist identity and witness. Or they may skimp on training altogether.

*"Our former interim pastor contributed greatly by running a harrow over the field. He detonated every land mine there was in the congregation."*

*"If we're not part of the solution, we're part of the problem. So what are we doing about calling and forming leaders?"*

*"There is such genuine love here for our pastor."*

### 7. Authority, Decision Making, and Structures

Where does authority lie in the church, and for which questions? This was a live issue everywhere we went in Canada. Some advocate for radical congregational autonomy, believing that the authority to discern ethical and doctrinal issues lies squarely with the local church. Others want regional and national levels of the church to take more authority, thereby providing more direction for local implementation of decision making. Still others advocate for some kind of combination, with ethical discernment, say, taking place in the congregation, but theological and doctrinal guidance being more broadly based. Finally, there are those who are simply inconsistent—advocating that central authority be imposed on others, while they enjoy more local autonomy for themselves.

Similarly, opinions vary around questions of congregational

structure and decision making. In some areas, congregations prefer a model in which few if any decisions come to the annual meeting of the congregation, other than those that

*"If in doubt, we do nothing."*

are legally required. Instead, the congregation frees the pastor, along with a "leadership board," to lead the congregation and make most of the decisions. Other models are more "democratic," where the whole congregation processes all decisions, including what color to paint the washrooms. During our tour, I was surprised at how many congregations have engaged, are engaging, or are planning to engage significant restructuring to adapt their governance to the demographic and social realities they face.

"It's been many years since we've voted on something in our congregation. If we can't come to consensus we haven't done it."

"We're great at sugar coating issues and then we pussyfoot around."

"Basically the key is to always have people think they are the front row in decision making."

"We're on board, but we still like to keep a stick in the spokes."

## *"We are open to change—a little bit."*

### 8. Volunteerism

Increasingly our congregations are having difficulty finding enough volunteers, whether committed Sunday school teachers, church council members, deacons, trustees, youth mentors and sponsors, or musicians. Repeatedly on our tour, we heard comments such as the following:

- "People don't want to commit to a three-year term."
- "If we get folks involved in occasional projects, they will more willingly commit to participate."
- "People are willing to help, but they don't want to be in charge."
- "Our folks are so very busy; we just can't make regular commitments anymore."
- "How can we compete with minor hockey, swimming lessons, dance classes, and the many options for involvement that there are in our communities?"

In response, many congregations are looking to streamline their structures so that they involve fewer people on fewer permanent committees.

We heard about some notable exceptions, however. One small congregation has too many volunteers to fill seventy open positions. They are looking at restructuring to create *more* opportunities for committee work. When I asked them about their secret, they humbly stated, "We just enjoy getting involved in the work of the church." Another congregation has fifteen youth and adult Sunday school classes, each one with two committed teach-

## *"We have very willing horses sharing the load."*

ers. I asked them whether they had any trouble finding teachers, and they seemed perplexed that I would ask. They told me that every August their superintendent and assistant superintendent go through the membership list and determine which people should be given the *privilege* of teaching that year. They then go and *tell* these persons the good news, and it is considered an honour to be asked. "We seldom, if ever, have anyone turn us down," they said.

"There is no fatigue in our church that is dragging us down; there is buoyancy that is helping us a lot."

"We're good at passing the buck."

"We like our summers off from church."

"If you will become a member, you have to put your shoulder to the wheel."

## 9. "Missional Church"—Local and Global

The missional church paradigm that the national church has promoted since 2001 has had a dramatic impact on the life of our congregations. All area churches have done intentional revisioning and restructuring, nurtured by the missional church vision. As we discovered on the tour, many congregations have initiated processes that examine their lives, identity, purpose, history, priorities, and activities in light of this paradigm. These have gained new confidence in being Christian in our world, both in personal and in congregational life.

Some congregations have redesigned not only their ministry models and organizational structures, but also their physical facilities to be more aligned with their missional understandings. It is fair to say that the missional vision is mobilizing a massive attempt at renewal in virtually all parts of our denomination.

> *"Forgiveness doesn't mean one side is right; it means that there is a channel through which love can flow."*

> *"Somehow when we invite God's Spirit to work, it suddenly shows up and surprises us."*

> *"Our greatest strength could also be our greatest weakness. Newcomers could mess up our community."*

> *"The word missional confused us all; now we're recognizing across the street and forgot about around the world."*

It is too soon to gauge the fruit of this vision for our future. However, in these last few years, the slogan "from across the street to around the world" has captured well a challenge that deserves comment. Congregations are struggling to become more relevant locally, yet they clearly also wish to be globally connected. Many congregations are finding it a new thing to be missionally immersed in the local context in which they find themselves. Individuals may be very active in community affairs, but this does not necessarily mean that the congregation itself is recognized as active in the community.

Such churches are trying to find creative ways to be missional locally. For some, that means encouraging members to see their involvements in their vocations and community more

### *"We are the church to the strong, the healthy, and the converted."*

intentionally as being representative of the church. Others are seeking to harness individual initiatives of service and witness, blessing them as being "the church." Still others are seeking ways for the congregation as a whole to connect more intentionally with its own context.

"Our congregation is ecologically friendly. We could disappear without a trace. And no one would realize that we've been here or that we've left."

"We are getting mixed messages that maybe our concerns about ministry are more about our guilt than about the welfare of the community."

A predictable result of this new focus on "across the street" is that these efforts absorb resources, both financial and human. That means the congregations come face to face with their other passion, namely the desire to be globally connected. The push and the pull of these priorities present significant challenges for decision making.

*"We have a budgeting rule: 50 percent of our donations must go beyond the congregation. This has encouraged giving. We have no trouble meeting our budget. Our budget has almost doubled in the last eight years."*

*"This church has taken in people from so many different backgrounds and mixed them up and it works and it's great."*

### 10. Priorities and Strategies

As congregations clarify their missional vocation and restructure accordingly, they are recognizing their need to fine-tune the ways they set priorities and budgets. With a plethora of ministry options at their fingertips, congregations understand that they must be more intentional about defining priorities and then using these as grids for decision making. Responding to funding requests because "it's my grandchild" or "she's from our congregation" or "they do good," is increasingly unsatisfying because the outcomes are difficult to gauge and impossible to monitor. Such loose decision-making processes often remain in place, however, because the congregations still have not adequately agreed on their priorities and strategies. At the same time, congregations are increasingly aware that choices will need to be informed by their covenantal commitment to other parts of the church, by their missional identity and principles, and by the priority of strengthening the church.

*"The ship [church building] is built; now we need to sail it."*

"At our annual meeting, I can holler at people and everyone takes it very well."

"Past experience has taught us that we can't know the future."

"We've made course corrections, but we've not been entirely reborn."

## Where To from Here?

From these observations, I hope it is clear that to be the church in Canada is exhilarating. On the one hand, it is challenging, perplexing, frustrating, and disheartening. But I also see abundant joy, significant community, deep commitment, energized vision, and tenacious persistence. The challenges I have identified are significant, and they will not easily be resolved. But even as we address them, there are some important things that we can and must do as a church if we are to experience God's blessing. I conclude these reflections with five things that each person in the church and each congregation can and should do now:

1. Pray for each other across the church. Make a special point of praying for congregations, leaders, and persons in a region different than your own.
2. Talk to each other—often. Find ways to build relationships with others in your own congregation, but also with people and congregations beyond your circle.
3. Visit each other. I hope we can facilitate cross-country exchanges for ministry and relationship building. But don't wait for others to initiate such visits. Your congregation has the capacity to begin that right now.

4. As a congregation, be intentional in the ministries you engage and the decisions you make. *Decide* to become a more active congregation in the larger church body across Canada. Don't assume this will happen by itself.

5. Contribute your strengths to others and be open to allowing others to help with your weaknesses. There are many gifts that, if offered and received in our body, will serve to strengthen us all.

*"Some in our congregation are stepping on the gas and some are stepping on the brake, and a vehicle needs both to function properly."*

# 3

# Unity and Diversity

On the God's People Now! tour, we heard and experienced a wide range of opinions, preferences, theologies, and ministries. We are indeed diverse. We worship in thirteen different languages on Sunday mornings. Of the 230 congregations in Mennonite Church Canada, forty-three use neither English nor German as their preferred language of worship. We visited three congregations in one area that among them are conducting services in nine different languages every week.

Age and demographic bulges appear in virtually every congregation. Educational levels within and among our congregations vary widely, as do vocational choices. Variations of size and class bring distinctive challenges. There are theological differences often expressed in worship styles, music, and teaching. Some in our church wonder whether women should be allowed to cut their hair, while others wonder whether same-sex marriages should be blessed by the church.

Yet all these folks function within the same church. Each one is aware of the diversity that is among us and at our own doorstep. Living with dif-

*"I'm not sure we like each other, but we do care for each other."*

ferences is an everyday experience in our church. In many ways, we take differences for granted and we do well at living with cultural and demographic diversity. In one congregation they openly acknowledged that they were about thirty years behind the times, but one of its members said, "It's a good place to be. That way we can watch all the errors our neighboring churches are making and we can avoid making the same ones." They were fully aware that they share the same communion table with their daughter congregation four kilometers away, a congregation that attempts to be fully up-to-date, while they purposefully remain thirty years behind.

## Common Ground or Grounds for Worry?

We observed that some people are nervous about the diversity and wonder what holds us together. MC Canada experiences distrust among people and misperceptions among congregations especially in attempting to deal with fundamental understandings of how to interpret the Bible for our faith and practice. In working at accountability among congregations and leaders, sharp disagreements occur between advocates of radical congregational autonomy and advocates of centralized authority.

> "As long as we stay away from some topics like politics and theology, we get along okay."

There is diversity and difference in our church; there is also hurt and deep pain within our body. There is also a deep yearning for health. How we do and prefer to do things often generates conflict. Tradition rubs against innovation and experimentation. We read the Bible differently and don't always agree on how to apply what we have learned from the Bible.

What excited me most about my visits to our congregations was my discovery—rather, my rediscovery—that there is in fact a great deal of unity in our churches on the things that really matter. There is ample and sufficient common ground among us that can serve as a foundation for whatever challenges of diversity that we may be facing. This is good news. Our challenge is to learn to take full advantage of this common ground in moving forward as God's people.

> *"I remember that congregational meetings once were difficult, and now I like everyone here. It takes the life right out of the meetings."*

Let me identify some key elements of this solid common ground that is present among us and that we can and must learn to trust.

- We believe in God and we believe that God has called us as individuals and as a church. We believe sincerely that we are responding to God's call in our lives. We need not distrust others in this, not even when they say it in different ways than we might.
- We are sincerely trying to be faithful disciples of Jesus, allowing his lordship to guide our lives. We need not distrust others in this, not even when our understandings of how it applies may lead to a diversity of opinion and action.
- We are convinced that the Holy Spirit is within and among us and that we are responding to the Spirit's transforming power in our lives. We need not distrust others in this, even when we discern differing behaviours that arise out of this conviction.
- We are committed to using the Bible as our guide to faithful living and believing. We need not distrust others in this, even when they read and interpret the biblical witness differently than we do and place a higher priority on some voices from the Bible than we do.

- We are deeply concerned about strengthening the church in its vocation to be God's people now. We yearn to be in communion with each other and to be the body of Christ in our context. We need not distrust others in this, even when they critique the church for its failures or blindly praise the church for its successes.
- We deeply believe that God is patiently desiring and seeking to have a saving relationship with us and that, as God's people, we need to mirror this desire as we relate to each other and to others. We need not distrust others in this, not even when they foster relationships with persons that we do not.
- We believe that God loves us deeply and also loves the created world so much that God has given his son to reconcile, redeem, and restore us and the world to the way we were meant to be. We also believe that we have been called to be witnesses to that redemptive love in how we are and in how we live. We need not distrust others in this, even when others demonstrate such reconciling love in ways that we do not.

Even those who worry about our unity would admit that differences among us have created no breach in our common commitment to these foundational pillars of unity. I believe this is because these foundations are not of our making. They come from our walk with God and they come from the grace of God among us. This is consistent with what we read in Ephesians. There we see that our task is not to *create* unity but to "maintain the unity" that comes from God (Ephesians 4:3). We see in this passage that ultimately we are not the authors of unity: God is. Our differences will not destroy the unity that God generates in the church. And this is good news.

*"I can relate to you because you're honest."*

## The Issue Is Trust

So why does it feel sometimes as though there is disunity? My visits have convinced me that the disunity we sense is not a lack of common ground. We have plenty of that, and what we have is sufficient. The issue, as suggested in each of the points above, is trust—or lack of it. Some of us don't trust that the other is taking seriously the same common ground that is so dear to us. When we differ on how we read the Bible for guidance, for example, we begin to suspect that the other is not reading it at all, or at least is not taking it seriously. When others understand things differently, we suspect that Jesus is not Lord of their life. When others behave differently, we suspect that the Holy Spirit is not transforming their life. When others prefer different music in church, we suspect that they do not want to worship God at all. When others speak out, we suspect that they do not have the strength, health, and welfare of the church at heart.

## "We're comfortable with the tension of the gray."

The good news is that underneath our differences and the distrust that often results, there is enough common ground to allow us to move forward as God's people now. We agree on foundational things even when we disagree on what to do with them. Our key task, then, is not to generate common ground but to cultivate it and to trust that it is already there, even when we disagree.

I now understand better why we are instructed in Ephesians 4:3 to "maintain the unity" that is among us, not to create the unity on which we want to stand. Unity is a gift of God's grace. Our task is to accept this gift and to work at its maintenance. Discerning God's will for the church is one of the key tasks of maintenance. It is at the core of what it means to be the church.

It is the calling to which we have been called. And our very best efforts to do this will have to be good enough. We cannot do more, and we should not do less.

Our diversity actually serves as a gift: it reminds us of Paul's description of our human condition: "Now we see in a mirror, dimly. . . . Now I know only in part" (1 Corinthians 13:12). This may indeed be the most important common ground that unites us all: namely, that God is God and we are not. We see things dimly, we know things only in part, and that is why we may well disagree with each other.

> ### "It would be great to work with black and whites, but that's not the world we live in."

Rather than disheartening us, therefore, our imperfect vision should point us to the grandeur and the wisdom of God. God's greatness within our human frailty is a reason to "bear with one another . . . forgive each other . . . with love" (Colossians 3:13-14) when we do disagree in spite of our agreements. We in the church are called together to pray, discern, share, give and receive testimonies of God's grace, decide what to do, forgive, forbear, admonish, bind and loose sin, love, and confess—all in a context of gratitude. Despite our differences, we can all praise God for inviting us into this huge privilege to be God's people for the twenty-first century in Canada and in the world. Our vocation is to be God's people, building relationships, standing on common ground in the midst of difference, affirming our unity because of our diversity (not in spite of it), and embracing our vocation as agents of transformation that aligns with God's reign already in our midst.

## Conclusion

Our congregations exemplify an amazing capacity to live with difference. Difference and diversity do not destroy the unity and the oneness we have with each other. In many ways, the differences unite us even more deeply. That is, when we stop to appreciate our differences, we become profoundly aware of the things that bring us together. Those things that unite us are more important than the differences that are so evident. Furthermore, the things that bring us together are gifts of faith, trust, commitment, and grace that come from God. It is profoundly comforting to know that what we long for most is not ours to give but ours to accept.

Everywhere, in every congregation we visited, we found mountains of goodwill nurtured by the golden hearts of members wanting to be God's faithful people. Mennonite Church Canada is sincere, well intentioned, and eager to be an effective agent of God's gospel in our world.

I would call on everyone in our church, especially those who wish to participate in important discerning processes, to ensure that our diverse passions and pronouncements are predicated on ground that is common among us. If we can do this, then we can continue to be the church. The list in Ephesians 4:4-5 can serve as an excellent starting point: there is one body and one Spirit, one hope, one Lord, one faith, one baptism, and one God. The purpose of the diversity of gifts of the Spirit is to arrive at a "unity of faith." We need to express this unity in multiple ways.

# 4

# What About the Young Adults?

The first and most consistent demographic pattern we observed on the tour was the thin presence of the eighteen- to twenty-eight-year-olds (young adults) in the active life of the congregations. There are only a handful of congregations that reported a significant demographic bulge of people in their twenties. Of course, my ears perked up when I encountered those. More frequently, there is average-to-good participation of teens in high school and then a sharp drop-off of young adults. What is happening?

Some things are obvious. Many young adults move away from home to work or study. If they stay, they have outgrown the youth group but don't yet feel that they belong with the adults. Many are single and don't fit into the young-married category. They are at an age where they want to keep their options open, rather than commit to long-term tasks. Their new jobs or schools, even if they are Christian schools, do not necessarily pull them into congregational life.

But there is much more involved than these issues. In one congregation that did have a significant number of active members in their twenties, I asked the young adults what the *"The power of children to draw in their parents is what we're seeing here."*

secret was. What attracted them to participate in the life of the congregation? Their answers, in summary, are instructive:

- They see their congregation addressing the issues of the day in relevant and practical ways.
- They sense that it's okay not to have easy answers and final conclusions in worship and study.
- Their pastor doesn't pretend to understand everything and know it all, and they see that as good.
- They have a sense of community with each other as they struggle through complex issues of faith and of church life.
- They find a strong theological home in the church but are allowed to wander and search.
- Their congregation encourages lay leadership; their creative involvement and initiative are genuinely welcome.

## "If I'm with a young person then I'm young, and when I'm with an older person then I'm old."

The things that they did not mention may be just as important. They are not asking the congregation to do more for them or to have more programs for them. Rather than expecting their church to have a college and career program, they seemed more interested in being integrated into all of congregational life. They do not want their congregation to have a "retention strategy" to hold on to them. Interestingly, the group with whom I spoke was not preoccupied with musical styles (at least they did not bring that up). In their congregation, the music style is actually quite traditional and conservative by some standards. I have tested the experiences of this congregation more broadly with others, and it seems that these young adults accurately articulate what many others feel.

> "I believe the older people are happy we're here,
> but they just don't know how to show it yet."

I have reflected a lot on what the church, as a system, offers to its young adults. The perception often is that it doesn't do very much. The truth is that enormous amounts of energy, time, and financial resources are invested for their benefit. Many congregations have pastors specifically dedicated to the needs of youth and young adults. There are four post-secondary Mennonite educational institutions related to Mennonite Church Canada that hope to serve young adults and prepare them for life and leadership in the church. Congregations and area churches have bursary and scholarship funds available. MC Canada gives significant grants to institutions and candidates for ministry through our budget and the Company of 1000, a fund established by MC Canada to support the training of pastors. All area churches have extensive camping programs that provide opportunity for leadership development and the deepening of faith commitments. The church commits funds to develop curriculum for this age sector. In financial terms, the investment the church makes to the faith formation of young adults adds up to many millions of dollars annually. Indeed, it is likely that it is the largest investment the church makes in any area of ministry.

And yet my sense is that young adults are not seeking more programs, more resources, or more creative worship. In fact, they sometimes perceive these things to be peripheral to their deeper concerns. Rather, they want to be heard, not just listened to. They are searching for church life that is deeply relevant to their social context, biblically prophetic, profoundly theological, globally aware, ecologically conscious, strongly communal, and full of integrity and passion.

## *"It's easy to welcome people; to embrace them is challenging."*

Young adults yearn more for authenticity in the life of the entire congregation than for ministry focused narrowly on their particular age sector. Their search reminds me of the

*"Seems like every age group in this church feels left out."*

instructions given to the people of Israel as they prepared to move into their new homeland. The words of the Shema are a reminder to all of us in the church to keep our priorities straight:

> Hear, O Israel:
>   The LORD is our God, the LORD alone.
>       You shall love the LORD your God with all your heart,
> and with all your soul, and with all your might.
> Keep these words that I am commanding you today in
>   your heart.
>       Recite them to your children
>       and talk about them when you are at home and
>           when you are away,
>           when you lie down
>           and when you rise.
>       Bind them as a sign on your hand,
>       fix them as an emblem on your forehead,
>       and write them on the doorposts of your house and
>           on your gates.
>                     —Deuteronomy 6:4-9

*"We have to fight for the front seats because the youth are always there."*

# 5

# Seniors and the Future of the Church

In one congregation, several teenagers and several women in their eighties came to our meeting. We experienced a remarkable intergenerational "love-in." The young folks were very sensitive to the musical tastes of the older folks and were very concerned that the drums and guitars not be too loud for them. The older women encouraged the young people and wanted them to be able to praise God in ways that were meaningful to them.

When we prodded more deeply about this harmony, one of the older folks said, "It hasn't always been like this. About twelve years ago we experienced an ugly split in our congregation. We learned from that, and we are determined that this won't happen again."

I was inspired. These seniors were willing to set their sails at different angles when the winds changed direction. They were willing to initiate change in the corporate culture of the congregation.

But the teenagers too have been transformed. They eagerly admitted that their worship band was actually playing more traditional hymns in the worship service.

"Are you learning to love the older hymns?" I asked.

"No, not exactly," replied one young woman. "It's not that we're learning to love the hymns more, but we have learned to love the seniors more, and they love the hymns and that's why we enjoy playing them."

It is remarkable that

> *"The fifty-five-plus generation is putting up its feet a bit too fast."*

when identifiable groups begin to struggle for well-being and guard the rights of groups other than their own, the spirit of the congregation changes.

In one congregation, a teenage girl prefers to attend her grandparents' small, rural, and aging congregation rather than the urban congregation of her parents. She has few peers in this rural congregation, and it means driving about an hour rather than going to the big, modern, easily accessible, and impressively programmed congregation where her parents attend. Why does she do this? "The seniors in this congregation love me and encourage me," she simply responded.

Present-day seniors, those born before 1946, and the baby-boom generation, born between 1946 and 1964, have an enormous opportunity to shape the ongoing possibilities of our church. The spirit displayed by these members will increasingly determine the health and potential of our church.

## "Even though we're dying, it's important that we live well until we die."

The demographic trend of Canadian society is similar to the church population. In the next twenty years, about 25 percent of the Canadian population will be in the senior stage of life (over sixty years). In MC Canada, 40 to 50 percent of our congregations currently have a senior demographic bulge. This will only increase as the baby-boom generation continues to age.

The image of a pig in a python helps us to visualize how the baby-boom bulge is moving through our society. If a python swallows a pig, the bulge will be evident in the snake. Because of the abnormal size of the pig, it will be possible to trace its progress as it moves through the long digestive process of the snake.

Similarly, the baby-boom bulge can be traced as it moves through our social system. It first put pressure on hospital maternity units when the boomers were born. Then they overflowed the public school system, leading to overcrowded classrooms, record construction, and double shifts of classes. It gave a huge boost to college enrolment. When the boomers reached child-bearing age, an echo boom of births fuelled the success of the minivan, saving Chrysler from bankruptcy. This "pig in the python" escalated the housing market in the early 1970s and is now stimulating the price of recreational property.

The oldest boomers turned sixty in 2006. This is the leading edge of about ten million Canadians who will be in the senior category in the next twenty years. The predictions of experts have materialized.

Let me suggest a few implications of the increasing numbers of seniors in our church.

- At times we are apologetic about being an aging church, and we talk disparagingly about it as something we need to "put up with." This attitude will need to change. We will need to embrace our aging as a gift if our church is to remain active and vibrant. A strong church cannot be built on apologetic attitudes. Strength must be built upon strength, and if the seniors are our strength for the foreseeable future, we need to affirm and build on that reality.
- The health of our church will depend on the spiritual health and the encouraging spirit of the seniors. It is unrealistic to think that our spiritual health can be good if the health of the seniors is not. Seniors and upcoming seniors need to be fully aware of the impact that their spiritual health—or lack of it—will have on the future of our church.
- The financial health of our church will depend on the generosity of seniors. If existing and beloved ministries are to continue, this group will need to be very intentional about its commitment to keep the church and its ministries strong. Seniors will not be able to hand off this responsibility to the following generations and expect the same financial power from fewer numbers. Seniors will need to model the importance of supporting denominational causes in the midst of personal and congregational decision-making processes.

- Seniors will need to be intentional and proactive in nourishing a positive and affirming spirit in church life. If they are not, the results will be very serious. Younger families, young adults, youth, and children will come, stay, or go depending on the encouraging spirit generated or not generated in the church by this group. If seniors have not yet learned how to be proactively affirming, they will need to learn.

- Seniors will have the power to resist, block, or promote needed change in the church. They will need to err on the side of encouragement rather than on the side of critical discouragement. One person commented to me: "If it's true that the CEO has to sign on to needed change for it to be successful, in our congregation the CEO is the seniors group. Nothing much can happen here unless they sign on."

- Initiatives and energy to ensure intergenerational harmony in the church will need to come from the seniors. Whenever there is an imbalance of influence, initiatives for harmony must come proactively from the majority group—in this case the seniors. If this majority is not proactive, it will be perceived to be resistant, thus severely damaging the life of our church.

- Seniors should not plan on putting up their feet too soon. The refrain we hear so often—"We've made our contribution; now it's their turn"—will need to be more nuanced, less definitive, more flexible and adaptable. The church will continue to need the gifts and the active involvement of the seniors. The new refrain should be, "This is what the ongoing but creative ministry of the seniors in the church looks like."

- Studies show that seniors who have grandchildren in the congregation have a more positive and affirming attitude toward the participation of the younger generations than those who don't. However, an increasing number of seniors will not have grandchildren in the congregation. This means seniors will need to cultivate their capacity to embrace children of other families and shower them with the same patience and love they would give to their own grandchildren. Seniors will need to demonstrate a hospitable attitude to the young, even when their own grandchildren are not present.

It will be tempting for seniors to want to participate in church life as consumers, that is, seeking and focusing on the personal benefits of church membership and involvement. They will be tempted to import societal norms into their participation in the church and exercise their sense of entitlement to their rights. Clearly, the church should and will need to pay attention to the special pastoral needs of seniors. However, the seniors should not see themselves primarily as consumers of benefits or as entitled benefactors, but as gifted, positive contributors to the life and well-being of the church for others. The church needs to be encouraged by the presence of the seniors, not only for what the church once was but also for what it can still become. The presence of the senior members needs to be a presence of wisdom and blessing and one that equips the church for the future of its challenging vocation.

*"Here, as long as anyone wants to chair, they are welcome to do so for as long as they want."*

*"Challenge for leadership will be to get us old fogies off our butts to do something."*

And we can take heart. What I have described is already happening in some congregations.

One congregation wanted to encourage more participation by young people. The younger folks responded enthusiastically by forming a worship band. They bought equipment: drums, guitars, amps, and microphones. The seniors were incensed and feared that the volume would be too high and the music would be unfamiliar. One older woman was especially critical.

The day came when this new worship band made its debut. They did very well. After the service, the same critical woman sidled up to the teenage leader of the group and whispered in his ear that if the group needed more microphones or other equipment, she would secretly finance it. Her changed sensitivity to the needs of the younger folks influenced her peers, which in turn heightened the sensitivity of the congregation.

In an urban congregation, a large group came out to meet us. Key representatives of most age and ministry groups in the church were present. There was a great spirit. An older gentleman spoke: "In this congregation, the seniors are the most active and most organized group in the church. And it's a great church."

"And what does your group organize around?" I asked.

His response was immediate and enthusiastic. "First of all, we are well organized for *visitation*. We feel it's our task now to take some of the visitation pressure off of the pastors. There are too many of us, and there's no reason why we can't support each other through regular and good visits. Second, we are organized to let the pastors know about any urgent or specific *pastoral needs* there may be among the seniors. Third, we are organized to *pray*; but we don't just pray generically. We pray for and with persons, groups, ministries, and initiatives in our church and beyond. It is so great to be able to uphold others in prayer. Fourth, we are organized to *serve*. We do what we can and where we can so that the community life of the congregation can prosper. We feel that although there are things we can no longer do, there is ministry that is critical to being the church that we can now actually do better. We are so grateful to be here."

# 6

# Leadership in the Church

There is a sense of restless yearning that things should or could be better in the church. And more often than not, it is assumed that good leadership could make things better. What is it that leadership is supposed to resolve? The answers vary, but when compiled they form a veritable litany of hopes, desires, and woes. We hear that leaders are needed who

- are more Anabaptist;
- are more relational;
- attract young people and young adults;
- have an attractive, inspiring, and articulate vision for the church;

*"Our pastor sees the forest but also sees every individual tree."*

- are bolder and more capable of successfully leading the church through change;
- are more creative;
- can reverse the demographic challenges in our churches;
- can stop the depopulation of some areas, attract large numbers of folks into the church, and encourage young people to stay in the community;
- are more passionate and can speak more from the "heart";
- are more spiritual;
- can make the Bible come alive and become more relevant and inspiring;

- understand organizations and how to lead and transform them;
- are younger;
- can mentor and encourage others in the church to become engaged;
- can empower the gifts of each person in the church for ministry;
- can "grow" the church;
- can make the church more multicultural;
- can be good teachers and preachers.

At the same time we also heard about the conditions that must be in place for leaders to be effectively developed for the life of the church. And this is another litany, including the following:

- It must not take too long to train leaders.
- It must not be expensive.
- It must be on-site so that leaders don't need to travel or move elsewhere to receive training.
- It must be readily accessible with flexible schedules.
- It must not be simply academic training, but needs to be hands-on and practical.
- It must be relevant to the life and ministry of the congregation.
- It must not be "narrow."
- It must not be "broad."

These litanies are complex, challenging, and to some extend contradictory. And so I wonder: how do we as congregations, area and national churches, address the need for leadership in our congregations and organizations? Let me offer some simple responses to what we heard.

- Not all the maladies of the church are a reflection of the quality of its leadership. We are living in a time of unprecedented social change, and these changes impact and shape the church. Many of the demographic realities of our society, for example, are not within the immediate control of leadership. So one of the important tasks for the church is to discern carefully what is and what is not within the potential of leaders to resolve.

> "When our pastors left, we were like on a boat that was sinking."

> "We bring the lamb to slaughter [pastoral evaluation] and ask whether we'll swing the axe or not."

- In some cases, the task of leadership is to help the church *resolve* the challenges that face us. In other cases, leadership cannot resolve but needs to help the church *address* its challenges. It is important for the church to discern carefully when we need to work toward resolution and when we need to address what we face as well as we can.
- An overarching need is that the church must become much more deliberate, intentional, and articulate about "being the church" than it has been under the Christendom assumptions that have shaped us. Christendom has taught us that it is legitimate to define the "church" according to geography and/or biology. In other words, "church" are those that live within a region or are born with certain ethnic or cultural identities. While the "believers church" tradition has denied the validity of such definitions, the truth is that we too have been heavily influenced by them. One of the qualities that needs to be a high priority for future leadership will be the capacity to help the church be

more intentional and articulate as it develops and makes decisions based on its identity and purpose rather than on ethnicity and geography.

- It became evident to me in these visits that congregations cannot take anything for granted in terms of their commitment to denominational identity and being part of the larger body of Christ. Congregational members will not develop an Anabaptist or Mennonite identity unless local leadership intentionally designs ways of shaping and teaching that. And congregations will not automatically understand the importance of belonging to a broader expression of the Mennonite church (whether the area, the denomination, or the global church) unless this too becomes an important and intentional part of the teaching and focus of the congregation. Broader identity beyond the congregation will not develop unless it is deliberately and intentionally fostered and nurtured at every opportunity. I have seen examples where leadership lives and breathes such broader identity and, amazingly, the congregation embraces this as well. Unfortunately, I also encounter many congregations where such identity is either taken for granted or is unimportant, and in those cases the congregation develops such an ethos as well. Not being deliberate is indeed deliberately shaping the church in a predictable direction.

- There is no "quick fix" in leadership development. It has always required effort, sacrifice, time, resources, and experience, and will continue to do so. And it will need to be a multi-faceted effort, with schools and congregations each playing critical, but different, roles in developing leadership for the church.

## *"When a new pastor comes, we'll be back to see what happens."*

Mennonite Church Canada has identified "growing leaders for the church" as one of the three priorities that needs urgent attention. The significance of this priority has been amply substantiated by my interaction

## *"There's no room for dictatorship around here."*

with congregations during these last months. May God give us the wisdom and patience to nurture the church via the path of nurturing leaders for it.

Perhaps it is the classic "Prayer of Serenity" that best expresses our desire to nurture the development of leaders in the church. I quote it here in its entirety, not only the few lines that are best known to us.

> God grant me the serenity to accept the things I cannot change.
> Courage to change the things I can, and the wisdom to know the difference.
> Living one day at a time; enjoying one moment at a time; accepting hardship as the pathway to peace.
> Taking, as He did, this sinful world as it is, not as I would have it.
> Trusting that He will make all things right if I surrender to His will;
> That I may be reasonably happy in this life,
> And supremely happy with Him forever in the next.
> —Reinhold Niebuhr

# 7

# The Role of the *Confession of Faith in a Mennonite Perspective* in the Life of the Church

My encounters with congregations during the tour have caused me to reflect a great deal on the impact of the *Confession of Faith in a Mennonite Perspective* in the life of the church. The *Confession* came up often in conversations, and references to it seldom lacked passion. Instead they were generally accompanied by some sense of strong conviction or pain. I share the following reflections with some degree of trepidation. What follows is not an objective academic study, but a personal reflection motivated but not limited by what I saw and heard.

The impact of our *Confession of Faith* depends on factors beyond the document itself. The sociological "location" of the *Confession* affects the impact it has in the life of the church, and its positive or negative impact often depends on whose hands it is in. It is like fertilizer. Good fertilizer in the hands of a Timothy McVeigh, for example, has a very different impact on society than the same good fertilizer in the hands of a Saskatchewan wheat farmer. The former uses it to build a bomb that will destroy lives, while the latter uses it to help feed the world. While this is perhaps too dramatic an example, I have become aware of how the *Confession*'s

*"I'm over-discerned."*

impact depends on the context in which it is used and on who uses it.

A few examples may help. It makes a difference when the *Confession* is in the hands of a pastor who understands that he has the authority of an "apostle" while others in the congregation do not. It makes a difference when leadership is understood in light of current business models, such as the "Carver" model. It makes a difference when the *Confession* is in the hands or a person steeped in the values of a workplace that is not intentionally modelled after a servanthood understanding of leadership, but who happens to be the chairperson of the elders in a local congregation. It makes a difference in the hands of a person who believes that careful biblical/ theological discernment in the body of Christ is a waste of time, but is leading the church council. It makes a difference in the hands of a pastor who is not a pacifist or in the hands of a church council that wants to acknowledge gay marriage as God-inspired. The impact and contribution of the *Confession* to the life of the church varies greatly depending on the hands in which it is found. There is, therefore, no one answer to the question of its impact on our church.

In some ways, the *Confession* has become a lightning rod and a shorthand way of affirming perceived directions of the denomination or of disregarding the denomination's relevance. It is helpful to see these responses as symptomatic of larger forces shaping our society and church. For example, people in North America struggle with the legitimate place and exercise of authority, both in society at large and in the church. The *Confession* is used in arguing for or against authority. Similarly, society argues about the legitimacy of the "establishment" and of "institutions"; the *Confession* can be a convenient tool to argue either for or against the denomination as an "institution." Our postmodern culture is ambivalent about the legitimacy or possibility of a "metanarrative," a common story and set of values that unites us all. The *Confession* is symptomatic of this struggle in our society. It is important to remind ourselves that the voices we heard may not adequately represent those that are less passionate and polarized.

This experience has led me to reflect on both the positive potential of the *Confession* in the life of the church and its "shadow side," as pointed to by its critics. I offer some of my reflections here.

## The *Confession* and the Bible

*Positive potential:* The *Confession* signals for us that the Bible needs to be interpreted precisely because its nature is such that it can be interpreted in multiple ways. The biblical interpretation of any confession can never claim to be the final and last word; it cannot replace Scripture. Rather, by providing an interpretation of Scripture, it signals the importance of the ongoing task of scriptural interpretation.

As unsettling as it is for some, there is no unmediated interpretation of Scripture, theology, or faith. Our understandings will be mediated through one lens or another. A confession articulates our best understandings and in the very act of doing so also signals that there are other interpretations that are worth considering. At its best, a confession roots us in a way that also opens us to each other. It is a foundation from which we want to explore the understandings of others. The confession functions both as an orientation and as a necessary point of reference for us.

*Shadow side:* Our *Confession* seems to have distanced us from ongoing serious, corporate, and joyful discernment of the Bible. Since the *Confession* has provided "answers," some unwittingly act as if there is no longer an urgent need to continue prayerful and careful discernment of the Bible. Some assume that continuing discernment is superfluous. For those whose preferences and biases are affirmed in the *Confession*, the desire to return to the biblical witness has evaporated. For those who find the *Confession*'s answers to be unsatisfactory, the biblical witness is now treated as irrelevant. In both cases, the study of the Bible and the need to implore the guidance of the Holy Spirit in our quest to be more faithful are viewed with suspicion and with cynicism.

## The Confession and Authority

*Positive potential:* The simple fact that we have produced a confession of faith is testimony that the Mennonite churches have successfully united to discern Scripture and experience in the body of Christ. This in itself signals the authority that God has granted to the church. That the *Confession* continues to be operative as a point of reference signals that authoritative interpretation has occurred, even though the *Confession* does not replace Scripture or the ongoing need to interpret Scripture.

*Shadow side:* For some, the *Confession* seems to have clouded the role of authority in the life of God's people. The Anabaptist understanding that the authority of the church rests in the discerning presence of God's Spirit within the body of Christ seems to be under siege. Many want unbendable authority to be exerted from human leaders, whether leaders in the national or regional church offices, or the elders or pastor within the congregation. And they want that authority to be exerted now. Waiting for authority to move through the prayerful body of Christ as it discerns Scripture under the guidance of the Holy Spirit is not compelling enough for many. Discernment seems to be something that has come to us from the past (as in the *Confession* of 1995) and this makes further discernment unnecessary in order to move faithfully into the future.

The *Confession* is not an infallible word of God to the church, yet many act as though it were. We must recover a better understanding of the notion of divine revelation in the world. God has revealed Godself in many ways. First, God spoke in creation: "And God said . . . and it was so . . . and it was good." Thus the creation itself, properly discerned, can be an important way of understanding some of the purpose and will of God. In Scripture, we hear God speaking through history and events, activities, and experiences in the lives of God's people. God's speaking was always discerned and interpreted within the people of God with the help of God's Spirit. God spoke through covenants and laws that were interpreted and applied in living contexts. Through prophets, God addressed pressing issues of faithfulness and sin. God spoke definitively through the living Word, the person and teaching of Jesus. God spoke through the "cloud of witnesses" that have gone before us and the "oral word" of those always trying to understand the will of God for their lives, even before texts were written.

"Change just kind of happens around here. I don't announce too many goals. I just implement them."

"If you work on something long enough, you can get it in the back door."

And, of course, God has spoken through the written word of Scripture, which has been foundational for God's people in its history. God spoke through the church's process of selection of some writings and not others to shape the canon (the Old and New Testaments) as a sufficient foundation for the life of the church. The understanding of this foundation is never exhausted and needs the ongoing discernment of God's people as they are motivated and guided by the Holy Spirit in their midst, discerning Scripture for whatever context in which they find themselves.

God's people have tried to articulate their understandings in compelling and understandable ways in liturgy, litany, creeds, and confessions. But these statements are not the primary authority for the church. We must consider seriously what has come before. But we must always be open to new insight, new discernment, and new understandings of the movement of God's Spirit in our midst.

It is evident that for some the *Confession* is being granted authoritative status that seems to negate the importance of other revelations from God that we have mentioned above.

# "We need to be happy with who we are and not try to be someone we're not."

## Virtue and Ethics

*Positive potential:* The *Confession* teaches that faith ultimately must be lived; it must be applied to the needs of people in whatever contexts they live. Scripture that is not relevant to our needs for life is not Scripture that is alive to us. The *Confession* reminds us that biblical faithfulness must be embodied in time and place. Communal efforts to discern how faith is to be lived are important, and the *Confession* is one of those important instruments designed to help us to do that.

*Shadow side:* The use of the *Confession* seems to have severely compromised some foundational virtues and gifts of the Spirit in the life of the church—virtues sorely needed in order to discern God's will for the faith and life of the church. The virtues of patience, forbearance, perseverance, and humility have been displaced in the eyes of many by an urgent need for definition, decision, immediate application, and implementation.

## Unity, Diversity, and Polarization

*Positive potential:* The *Confession* is an important and constant reminder that diversity, like change, is not a virtue in and of itself. It reminds us that diversity must build on common ground. We need to expend energy to strengthen the common ground on which the diversity of gifts of the Spirit can build. The *Confession* is one effort to define the common ground that we stand on. There is one body, one God, one Spirit, one Lord, one baptism, one faith, one hope upon which the Spirit pours out generous portions of gifted diversity.

*Shadow side:* Insofar as people use the *Confession* as a final divine word, as discussed earlier in this chapter, they help increase the polarization within our body. When they sideline other channels of God's communication, they obscure the nuances that we need to discover there. The *Confession* needs to be a tool that allows us to be flexible, not entirely definitive; humble and not too dogmatic; relationally compassionate and not doctrinally cold; more relational and less propositional; more contextual and less categorical. It needs to be a tool that encourages an ecclesiological perspective (based on discernment, belonging, and being) that informs our ethical (based on behaviour) concerns.

## The *Confession* and Discernment

*Positive potential:* A confession opens doors to further discernment because it provides a good platform from which to begin. The *Confession of Faith in a Mennonite Perspective* signals that although we are eager to know and understand more, we do not begin this quest from nothing. It sends the very important signal that the church has spoken and has done its best at discerning God's will. It also sends the signal that the church can and must speak again, knowing that any confession reflects a "glass dimly." Rather than close doors to discernment, therefore, it should allow discernment to take place in a non-threatening, serious, yet open manner.

*Shadow side:* The *Confession* is sometimes used as a screen to test biblical faithfulness rather than as a mirror that demonstrates that we all fall short of the glory that God has in store for the church. In our visits, we frequently heard statements that differ from the teaching of our *Confession*. Often such statements were uttered by the same persons who have a passionate concern about the "variances" of interpretations demonstrated by others. In one meeting I pointed to several statements made in the group that would clearly put that group at variance with the stated intent of the *Confession*. They disregarded their differences either because in their minds they were of a "secondary" nature or because they did not impact the "salvific" (saving) intent of God for the world.

The fact that no process for ongoing review was established when the *Confession* was accepted in 1995 is generating unease in our church. For those who like the document, any suggestion of ongoing discernment is immediately suspect. For those who don't like it, the lack of a review process makes the church increasingly irrelevant in their eyes. For them it seems as though the church is not engaged in fresh discernment for the contemporary context. On both sides, anxiety about updating the *Confession* blinds folks to the fact that discernment is healthy and that it is, indeed, the ongoing task of a faithful church.

## The *Confession* and Identity

*Positive potential:* The *Confession* is a reminder that the Spirit of God is still at work among us, allowing us to discern the will of God for the church and to do so corporately. This assures us that God is active and that we need not live in fear—fear that the Spirit of God has abandoned us; fear that faith is meaningless; fear that we might do the wrong thing. The *Confession* allows us to relax. God's Spirit is present. And God's Spirit still provides guidance for faith and life in the body of Christ.

*Shadow side:* I am surprised how much fear there is in our churches. We fear that we are not capable of good spiritual discernment. We fear that evil forces that threaten to overtake us are stronger than the Spirit of God at work within us. If we are confident of God's Spirit within us, we are afraid that the Spirit is absent from others in the church. In one meeting, one leader declared publicly that God's Spirit was not present in a particular congregation in a different region from his. What lies behind such a statement?

*"In our congregation there has been a lot healing that has happened, all of it closely linked to the study of Scripture and its application."*

"The Anabaptist vision is getting world-renown recognition, and we're going to be ashamed of it at home? No way!"

"Our struggle is to become real Anabaptists, even though we live among Mennonites."

Forces at work in our society (individualism, consumerism, pluralism, and autonomy) have made us less ecclesial, less "body" oriented and directed. The ongoing responsibility of the church to "discern the times" is suspect. The authority and capacity of the body of Christ to do spiritual discernment has been compromised. As a result, the joy of being and belonging to the church is no longer a priority. Ethics, ministry, activity, services, numerical growth, answers to difficult situations, and worship and music that suit personal preferences have all, to some degree, replaced the foundational joy of living in covenant, strengthening our identity, and engaging in corporate discernment.

### The *Confession* and the Mission of the Church

*Positive potential:* The *Confession* at its best is a proclamation to a watching world. Many today seek a compelling purpose for life. The *Confession* articulates such a purpose and in doing so attracts many seekers. Two examples will suffice. Leaders in the Vietnamese Mennonite Church have reported that the translation of the *Confession* attracted many newcomers and that the church owes part of its growth to the strong foundation that the *Confession* provides. A similar example is found in the Cuban church, La Iglesia Evangélica Misionera de Cuba. This denomination too reviewed many confessions in its search for meaning and being. It settled on our *Confession* as the one that most closely reflects how it wishes to shape its identity. Many similar testimonies come from other cultures and countries.

*Shadow side:* The impact of the *Confession* on mission needs to be undergirded by a community in which its application to the life of a people can be observed and experienced. Without such a connection, the potential of this form of witness is severely hampered. I hope that the shadow tendencies noted in this chapter will not be exported with the *Confession* as it is embraced by other languages and cultures.

**"Why are people wanting to get baptized? Because they want to part of a missional church."**

**"The more you practice love, the more love you get."**

**"We don't want to be welcomed; we want to be embraced. And there is a big difference."**

## Conclusion

It is critically urgent for our church to grasp the healthy role that the *Confession of Faith in a Mennonite Perspective* is meant to have and to avoid the shadow sides that weaken the church. It may be helpful to be reminded again how the *Confession* describes its own functions and roles. These are provided in its introduction and can be summarized as follows:

- The *Confession* provides guidelines for the interpretation of Scripture. At the same time, it is subject to the authority of the Bible.
- It provides guidance for belief and practice. A written statement, however, should support but not replace the lived witness of faith.
- It builds a foundation for unity within and among churches.
- It offers an outline for instructing new church members and for sharing information with inquirers.
- It gives an updated interpretation of belief and practice in the midst of changing times.
- It helps in discussing Mennonite belief and practice with other Christians and people of other faiths.

Even if this preamble is not as authoritative as the *Confession*'s twenty-four articles, it does articulate the church's best thinking at the time of its adoption. And it continues to be instructive for us today. May God be with us and help our continuing discernment of belief and practice.

## *"God works in ways we don't even think and know about."*

# 8

# The Calling of the Church

Spiritual imagination is likely the most powerful yet underutilized resource of the Christian church. Consistent failures of imagination have led to church splits, intransigence on issues, power struggles, and the perception that the church is an irrelevant institution in today's world. But in thousands of small ways, imagination has also sparked renewal movements, creative ministries, and dynamic faith. Imagination generates hope because it suggests that things don't need to be the way they are. And hope generates energy and effective ministry.

The congregations that we visited demonstrated many signs of creative imagination. The quotes I gathered point to much that is healthy, effective, and strong. Often these insights sharpen scriptural images about the church and God's vision for it, and as such they too can spark our imaginations.

When we look at evidence in the Bible, in our history, and in our contemporary world, it is clear that the world and human experience within it are not yet what they are meant to be. The biblical witness itself is framed by two images of how things

*"We are our own worst enemies by making cultural things Mennonite."*

should to be. The garden of Eden is a glimpse from the beginning of time, and the New Jerusalem come down to earth offers a glimpse from the end of time. If we compare these two images with our reality and the reality of our history, we note a dramatic gulf between where we have been, where we are, and where we should be. This gulf includes the persistent presence of violence, poverty, racism, war, crime, greed, ecological exploitation, abuse, injustice, and hunger. These realities characterize neither how we once were (Eden) nor how we will one day be (New Jerusalem). We live in the in-between time in which God is working to restore the world to the designs for which it was intended.

Scripture tells us, and in faith we believe, that we are witnesses to and participants in an enormous and cosmic, divinely orchestrated restoration project. This raises some important questions. If the world is being restored, what are the strategies God prefers to use to do so? What participation, involvement, and contribution does God expect from us?

The answers to these questions are succinctly and profoundly articulated in the letter to the Ephesians. The primary strategy God wants to use to restore the world is incarnation, that is, God becoming flesh in human history. This strategy means that a peoplehood of God needs to be formed and nurtured (see Ephesians 1:22-23; 3:10; 3:19; 4:1). This peoplehood has proven to be an interesting assortment of apostles and apostates, saints and sinners, losers and winners who are empowered by the gifts of the Holy Spirit and who try to model their life after Jesus of Nazareth. They lurch forward, and sometimes backwards, seeking to reflect the intentions of God's reign and the person, Jesus, whose life and witness provides a glimpse of what was and what is meant to be.

What does God require of us in this restoration project? Ephesians gives us some remarkably clear guidelines. First, we are to trust and believe that God's strategy of incarnation will actually work in the struggle against evil and in the restoration of all things. This means that our imaginations must work overtime, because it is not easily evident that this can be possible. Ephesians refers to this as the "eyes of your heart enlightened" (1:18). But simply believing this is not enough. We must also commit ourselves to the primacy of God's peoplehood—establishing, nurturing, and mobilizing it in every cultural context. This way, God's restoration and reconciliation become actual alternatives that can be seen, touched, and felt in the world. We need to get serious about God's strategy and actually make it our own priority.

## *"Why have we grown? We understand what we believe, embrace it, and then push our limits."*

### Biblical Focus

It is exciting to see how Ephesians focuses the vision and strategy of peoplehood for us. The letter begins by summarizing God's ambitious intention: "To gather up all things in [Christ], things in heaven and things on earth" (1:10).

"Gathering up all things in him" is not a modest goal. It is a staggeringly massive undertaking. "All things in heaven and things on earth" underlines the vast scope of the intent of this restoration process. Another way of saying this is that there is nothing that is not included in God's dream for restoration. There is no limit, no boundary to God's reconciling intent. If God's strategy is to work through peoplehood, this also means that there is no agenda that is not the agenda of the church.

We tend to limit the role of God's peoplehood within this restoration project. Secular society tends to relegate the church to a role of chaplain, a role that is blessed by Christendom-minded governments and civil society and is acceptable to the political correctness of pluralism. God's people are often considered either fringe radicals or irrelevant relics. As a church, we have often accepted this limited role and lived contentedly within it. But in light of this broad statement of intent in Ephesians, such reductionist and limiting tendencies for the role of the church can only be described by one word: heresy. There is nothing that is not included in God's restoring and reconciling work, and therefore there is nothing that is not included in the agenda of God's people.

> "Telling and retelling stories of grace we have experienced creates a culture of grace in our congregation."

> "As we feel better about ourselves, we're no longer afraid to invite others."

Ephesians goes on to say that God has acted on this intention by raising Christ from the dead, establishing his authority over "all things," and by making him the head of the body, the people-hood of Christ. "And he has put all things under his feet and has made him the head over all things for the church, which is his body, the fullness of him who fills all in all" (1:22-23).

Ephesians 1:17-22 gives us a description of the tools needed to understand God's intention for the church. These tools are a spirit of wisdom; a spirit of revelation; eyes of the heart that are enlightened; understanding of the amazing hope of our vocation and the wealth of the glorious inheritance among us; and the immeasurable supply of power that God makes available for this vocation. This is a cosmic collection of power tools to restore the universe! The source of power is God at work in Jesus, especially in the power of the resurrection. And this is the same power on which the body of Christ, the church, can count in its vocation of restoration.

There is a call here to understand that the church, with Jesus as its head, has more "power" than any ruler, authority, power, dominion, and any name in this era or any era to come. In other words, there are unseen resurrection forces ready to support the dream and vocation of reconciling the world, if we can only think big enough to engage them.

Often when we think about incarnation, we think about God becoming human in Christ Jesus. And this is indeed unique and important. But it is evident in the Bible that when God chose incarnation (becoming flesh) as the main strategy for restoring the world, this is not only a reference to the incarnation of God in Christ. It is also a reference to the incarnation of Christ in the church. The flesh of the body of Christ—the church—is also part of the incarnational strategy of God. And the Bible clearly indicates that the strategy of becoming flesh in peoplehood is not a new or post-Jesus strategy. It has been the foundational strategy from the beginning.

The entire Hebrew Bible—the Old Testament—focuses on God's attempts to form a peoplehood that is covenantal in character, communal in personality, and obedient by nature. There are many tendencies in our day that reduce the potential with which God has gifted the church. Many factors seek to diminish the intended role of the church as a foundational instrument for the restoration of the world. Such tendencies too are heretical in light of this passionate statement of the vocation and the potential of the church.

According to Ephesians, the power of peace and the potential of reconciliation and restoration are mysteries that were hidden but are no longer. Enemies can be reconciled. Walls can be broken down. Authorities of all sorts need to know and respond to this new potential. And the vehicle of communication to all authorities is the church: "So that through the church the wisdom of God in its rich variety might now be made known to the rulers and authorities in the heavenly places" (3:10).

This statement points to and defines the calling of the church. And this calling is not difficult to comprehend. However, it has proven to be very difficult to trust and believe. It is a profound vocation for the full reconciliation of our world with all its woes and its sin. It is a vocation for the church; that is to say, it is an ecclesial vocation of peoplehood.

*"The church is only as strong as the people it sends out."*

This is a calling that is all-encompassing, transformative, and prophetic—a calling that should be impossible to domesticate. Yet in spite of this profound articulation of the church's purpose, we have managed to tame the vocation to which we have been called. Some would say that the taming of the vocation has actually happened *because* of how powerfully the restoring intention of God has been expressed. Lack of imagination, neglect, and unbelief render the vocation of the church powerless. Even if we have comprehended this calling, we haven't trusted it to be foundational for our own strategic planning. Instead we have reduced the church's calling to correspond to what the church has become rather than to what it was meant to be. We must say again that reducing the potential that God has envisioned for and given to the church is heretical.

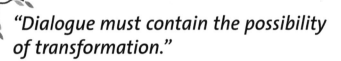

## "Dialogue must contain the possibility of transformation."

## "Don't take a position in the church because you should but because you want to."

God has already generated peace by showing that it is possible to form one humanity out of two hostile peoples—the Jews and the Gentiles (see Ephesians 2:13-19). Hostilities between two seemingly irreconcilable bodies have ended. Walls of division and separation have been broken down. And Ephesians goes on to outline other nitty-gritty examples of how this incarnational presence restores the world to its intended purposes. Wives and husbands become mutually accountable to each other and transform the nature of the home; children have parents who should be obeyed and parents have children who don't anger them, and thereby transform the nature of our social fabric; slaves and masters become one and transform the economic foundation of the world; privileged distinctions of gender disappear, and the negative potential for abuse is addressed; nations and ethnicities that once were hostile, separated, and enemies are

**"I am denomination- ally agnostic."**

now shown to be of one incarnation, transforming the potential of politics. Peace is accomplished via the cross, thus transforming our ethics, militaristic tendencies, and confidence in violence.

There is, in short, no part of the created and social world that is not targeted for restoration and reconciliation in this plan and intention of God. And the astonishing foundational strategy for such far-reaching and profound transformation is the formation of peoplehood. That is to say, it is incarnational. God's hopes and dreams will become flesh within an alternative society and a paradigm-busting community. This community will demonstrate that God's purposes are indeed viable and living possibilities. This is nothing less than the formation and the vocation of the church, the body of Christ, as an echo of Eden and a prototype of the New Jerusalem.

Most of us, I suspect, would agree that this is the incarnational vocation to which the Bible calls us. Yet many of us feel a certain sense of discomfort in talking about, owning, and embracing this vocation so openly. Why?

Our culturally sensitive souls object to embracing this biblical calling for two reasons, and it's important to mention them here. One is a sense that such a vocation sounds too presumptuous and triumphalistic. We would prefer to be more humble and more confessional—admitting our mistakes, acknowledging our inadequacies—and be content to modify our vocation and be more realistic. We are so very aware that the church has not modelled this vocation well, and we want to acknowledge our mistakes. The second objection is that in affirming this vocation, we feel that we are somehow not acknowledging as fully as we ought that God's activity is not limited to the church but that indeed God's reign extends beyond the limits of the church. Because we have friends of other faiths, we feel embarrassed claiming such a vocation for ourselves.

## *"People are more excited about this congregation than they are about God."*

These objections are valuable, but they must not replace or reduce the powerful vision for incarnational peoplehood that permeates the biblical witness. Indeed, when we compare this calling with the historical reality of the church, one cannot be presumptuous or triumphalistic. We *do* need to be confessional, and we *do* need to acknowledge that the divine invitation into such a calling is pure, unmerited grace.

Further, such a vocational vision does not limit God's activity to one strategy. We must never pretend that we can impose limits on what God does and how God chooses to do it. Rather, we rejoice and celebrate that God's intentions will not be stifled by a church with a reduced vision and a failing heart. Neither will God's intentions be stifled by our attempts to use strategies other than incarnational peoplehood. But having said that, we must continue to grapple with the calling and commit to it. Neither the confessional stance of the church nor acknowledging God's immeasurable workings beyond the church changes the foundational vision of God's incarnational strategy of peoplehood. In other words, confession, failure, and limitation should not lead to a reduction of our vocation but to a recommitment to it.

# 9

# Do We Really Believe?

In the previous chapter we were reminded of the powerful vocation for the church to which the Bible calls us. What practical difference should this make for us? This vocational vision suggests that our highest priority should be to imagine and work toward establishing, nurturing, and being incarnational "communities of salvation." [1] This would surely be a logical way of responding to God's invitation to participate in the reconciliation of the world. We need to imagine the possibility that each geographical, social, political, economic, human context in the world should be blessed with mature and discerning incarnational communities of salvation, that is, we should see the strengthening of God's peoplehood (the church) as our number-one priority for ministry. This kind of imagining would lead us to believe that the absolute highest priority for our decision making in terms of where to put our energies, how to spend our dollars, how to administer our assets, and how to develop our strategic plans would be to encourage the presence and strengthening of such assemblies of salvation. And what do assemblies of salvation look like? They are

- deeply rooted in every imaginable context,
- indigenous in character,
- living, applying, and contextualizing the values, the teachings, and the incarnation of our Lord,

*"If we need money, somehow it's just there."*

- continually discerning the signs of the times and their context from the perspective of God's will and way for the world,
- spiritually mature with the capacity to discern life-giving options based on the lordship of their master,
- creatively equipping and responding with the gifts that God has showered on them,
- profoundly prophetic yet compassionately priestly,
- deeply connected to what God is doing beyond their assemblies through other strategies and instruments,
- wildly hospitable and invitational, and
- humbly and meekly committing their lives to the new paradigm for life that, ironically, may be leading them to suffering.

Do we really believe that the paradigm-busting, all encompassing, alternative-generating, incarnational, reconciling/saving vocation of peoplehood (the church) is the foundational strategy of God for the transformation of the world: a strategy that should in turn inform our own priorities?[2]

I believe the answer is simple: we find this difficult to believe. We have seen the poor performance of the church and the way it has missed opportunities. We have experienced its tragic flaws and reduced vision, and these have contributed to our cynicism and scepticism about the potential of the church in the plan of God for transformation. This has led to the loss of nerve of the church itself. We have replaced the ecclesial vision that is so foundational in the Bible with many other strategies that appear to be more easily implemented, defended, and measured.

"We need to learn to love people we don't like."

So what is the antidote to our "loss of ecclesial nerve," to not having trusted in God's primary strategy for the "restoration of all things"? In the previous chapter we spoke of imagination and its power and potential to transform the church. It is imagination, the "eyes

*"Our congregation appears to be developmentally stuck."*

of the heart enlightened," that has the power to enable us to get past our guilt, shame, and failure and get on with actually being the church as God intended. We have already heard something of what imagination can do. In the introduction we heard from a congregation that imagined itself as a songbird and a seedbed church. Imagining the church in ways that are practical and speak to our context helps us to be the church.

Creatively imagining what it means to be the church has its beginning in the New Testament itself. In those sacred pages we have no less than ninety-six different images and word pictures for what it means to be the church. There is no one dominant image of the church, but rather an astonishing array of images, each one trying to capture something of the importance of the ecclesial vocation. The New Testament uses word pictures, describing the church as a boat, a bride, a lamp, a letter, a field, and a flock. And there are ninety more. No one of these images communicates the full range of the simplicity and complexity of the church's unique genius. Each image contributes to our understandings of the shape of the church: its structure, its composition, its purpose, its strategies, and its soul.

What is so striking about these word pictures is that we cannot derive a precise definition, an authoritative shape, or any one organizational structure for the church from them. This may be disconcerting for some. Therefore we are tempted to select only a few of the images, generate our structures around those, and ignore what the other word pictures are trying to teach us about being the church. Or we are tempted to suggest that if ninety-six images are good, then more must be even better. We thereby grant ourselves the license to organize the church in ways that don't take seriously the images that are there, and thus our imaginings go beyond critique and careful discernment about the profound vocation of the church.

*"We don't really plan much into the future. There is enough evil to deal with one day at a time."*

The church is most faithful when it tries to understand and implement what each image points to. The church is least faithful when it uses the abundance of images to justify its inactivity or its unaligned priorities, or when it uses the multiplicity of images to pretend that it doesn't matter what any one in particular wishes to communicate. The system of images in the New Testament takes for granted that the Holy Spirit is the permanent guest of the church. It is this Spirit of God who enlightens the eyes of the heart, gifts the church for ministry, educates for discernment, empowers it for resistance, and nourishes it for discipleship to Jesus. The Spirit is welcome in our boardrooms and our bedrooms; the Spirit is welcome in our bank accounts and in our recreational activities. The church's ministry of hospitality must be extended first to the Holy Spirit, opening all doors, structures, and discussions to the Spirit's presence.

*"We don't want to get into the habit of using our few resources only for ourselves, but to share what we have with others."*

These images ultimately are trying to express and understand the mystery of God. They are an attempt to encourage our belief in the vocation that God has given to the church. Those who first imagined these word-picture descriptions of the church did so out of the elation of having discovered something of the mystery of God for the church. This "imagination language" is useful to us only insofar as we also try to connect to the reasons for the excitement and the elation of the writers. To recapture the cause of the excitement is to recapture a grand design for our calling and ministry.

The church, as God's people and as the prolonged presence of Jesus on earth, is depicted as a vital instrument to promote God's justice, compassion, grace, and salvation to the world. The biblical writers had caught on to an exciting vision, and they tried to contagiously communicate what they had come to understand via images and the use of word pictures. As the church today, our task is to connect our imaginations to those of the scriptural writers to discover, discern, and delight in God's intentions for church today.

"How we get there is important."

# Appendix

# Wisdom, Humour, and Insights of *God's People Now!*

Art Linkletter, a friend of children, used to have a television program entitled *Kids Say the Darndest Things*. The core of the program was simply to listen to the way children speak and hear clearly what it was that they were saying. It was a delightful program. The wisdom of the kids was profound even though it was often humorous.

The core of this book is similar, except that we focus not so much on what kids say, but on what participants in our church have said. I was consistently impressed with the precision and clarity with which folks would focus a conversation, summarize an issue, and provide wisdom about the life of the church. These folks are the heartbeat of our church and therefore these quotes collected from them need to be the heartbeat of this book. This appendix contains a master list from which the quotes highlighted in the book are taken.

How were these quotes collected? We travelled with laptop computers. In each visit we requested permission to take extensive notes and indicated to those in the conversations that they may well find themselves quoted publicly. However, we also promised that they would not be identified, either by personal or congregational name. Whenever folks would utter these pithy and wise statements in the heat of conversation, we would make sure to jot down as exactly as we could what they were saying. While I would not guarantee that each quote is 100 percent exact, I do believe that each one accurately conveys what was intended. People were surprisingly open, vulnerable, and frank with us. We have not censored what people said. Affirmations and criticisms equally were noted. We have made no effort to align what people said with what we might have preferred to hear. The quotes provided are direct, all-inclusive, and, more often than not, poignant. Every single quote is worth savouring; is worth a cup of coffee with colleagues; and is worth reflection and extended conversation. It is the voice of our church. We need to hear and to listen carefully.

## *Quote Topics*

Church Growth
Culture and Change
Demographics
Denominational Comments
Essence and Identity
Intergenerational Dynamics / Youth and Young Adults
Leadership Development
Mission: Local and Global
Missional Church Impact
Polity, Authority, and Decision Making
Priorities and Strategies
Structuring for Effectiveness
Tour Comments
Unity and Diversity
Volunteerism
Worship and Music

*Church Growth*

"Our greatest ministry seems to be our cemetery; once family members are buried, the families begin coming to church too."

"Our rural church sometimes has an appeal of romance rather than faith to town people."

"We have an expectation that church life is meant to be lived with one another."

"The church will become who the planters are."

"We have to caution our members not to overwhelm new people who come with too much attention."

"How can we be a church if we don't have venues to interact with each other?"

"We have aches and pains because we're growing. These are signs that we are alive."

"It's important when there's bleeding to bind the wound."

"Our secret of survival is stubbornness."

"We have some of the worst funerals here at this church, and this brings new people into the church."

"If you always do what you've always done, you always get what you've always got."

"He suggested that our congregation would not grow, and then I'm afraid he experienced the wrath of grace from me. I'm sorry."

"Often new people invite new people more than old people invite new people."

"We are gathered to grow and scattered to serve."

"It's amazing how God blesses steps taken in faith."

"When I was hired, part of my mandate was to close down the German service. What has happened is that we've gone from 25 to 150 persons. So I guess I haven't really done my job."

"We are almost overwhelmingly acceptable and maybe draw people in too quickly."

"We're not a congregation full of rebels. But we don't turn anyone away."

"There is a form of resurrection that will come here."

"There is something here that wants to destroy us."

"Little puddles of impact are expanding."

"Neva, Neva, Neva give up. And we won't."

"Our church began to see the need for yieldedness as a survival issue."

"We did very little except pray for three months. God showed us a process to follow."

"Maybe we had stopped inviting new people to church and that was a problem."

"Your heart is where your benefits are."

"Let's let God decide."

"I had a problem. I needed to take sausage that shouldn't thaw and potatoes that shouldn't freeze. All through the meeting I kept going out to the car to change things around. I didn't focus as well as I should have."

"Coming to church is more positive than going to the coffee shop."

"Key to growth is theological honesty. We don't have all the answers; we don't have quick answers and don't pretend to have them. We are genuinely searching, and there is a lot of humility in our leadership."

"We're in a place that God is blessing us."

"This church is like a countdown for a rocket to go into space. We're just about to take off, and we're in for quite a ride."

"Growing is a good opportunity both to get hurt and to be blessed."

"Our building used to be a government liquor store, but now we're distributing a new kind of spirit."

 *Culture and Change*

"Change is a good thing, but we need to make sure where we're going to is better than where we've been."

"Change is difficult to plan and control. Somehow it happens."

"When you go through change, there will always be resistance."

"Maybe we're not smart enough to be discouraged."

"In this process of living with uncertainty, we do trust that we are being led."

"The older folks saw so much change that they looked deep into the heart of the values."

"You can't pull a tree out by the roots and say that's change. That's something else than change."

"Never use the word *change*."

"We're stupid old farts, and we need to get used to new things."

"We are in a world of abundance here where we cannot do very much."

"For many people now, their life is ministry and don't have time for more."

"Go ye into all the world, especially into every church, with the gospel."

"The advantage we have is that we are thirty years behind other congregations and we can see how things have gone, and so we don't walk as blindly as others seem to. We can learn from their mistakes."

"Spirited energy describes exactly what's going on in our congregation."

"We are satisfactorily dissatisfied."

"The danger of criticizing others is that you may have to do it yourself."

"We hanker after adequacy."

"Our congregation could never be faulted for rushing into things quickly."

 *Demographics*

"Our day trips are eight hours one way."

"Our biggest concerns have to do with what to do with our rapid numerical growth."

"Our Sunday school is at full capacity."

"We can hear the subway from our church, and that's a symbol of the transience of our church."

"I feel comfortable saying that our church is a dying church."

"Even though we're dying, it's important that we live well until we die."

"We are a seedbed church; other churches are harvesting what we sow."

"We're a fifty-five-plus congregation with arms open to those who don't yet meet that characteristic."

"It's an age thing; we're getting older; it's not a bad thing."

"How we treat our seniors in the next twenty years may be the most important thing the church will do."

"Older people want to see growth, but it's the changes that intimidate them."

"We could have another congregation made up of people who have been deported from our congregation."

"Don't worry about us being deported, because we go well discipled in the Lord."

"It's a long winter here, and new ideas are welcome."

"Our church is a loving church. Our decline is not our fault."

"Our congregation has served as a 'halfway house' for folks coming from other backgrounds."

"We were attracted here because there were older persons here."

"The old people here aren't as old as the old people in my former church."

"The churches in our community are kind of like hockey teams; we put people on waivers and then trade members with each other."

"The fifty-five-plus generation is putting up its feet a bit too fast."

"We've got one good thing going for us: we've extended our cemetery to take care of all of us."

"Transition will be a permanent part of life, and we need to learn to deal with transition."

"As a congregation, we want to survive."

"It's important that our church not become the flavour of the month."

"Auctioneers are doing well." (describing the agricultural reality).

"We have no tenors."

"Our church is going from a grape to a raisin."

"People just want to be heard."

"I had a brain-wave and someone asked me if it hurt."

"If you think of something to do, think of something that doesn't cost money."

"We have an agricultural problem, but we're not looking to the church to solve it for us."

"The church can't address the crisis in agriculture. The church can address the crisis in the lives of the people."

"The numbers of people in agriculture are the same as the numbers that are gay. We're in a very small minority. We feel very much misunderstood."

"The average farm income in Saskatchewan last year was minus thirty-seven thousand dollars."

"We have a stack of auction catalogues. That shows what this area is all about."

"The size of our congregation is our greatest weakness, but it is also our greatest strength."

"Look how things have changed: where are the men today?"

"We may have the distinction of being the only Mennonite church in Ontario located only on gravel roads."

"We're aging, but most folks here are still on the green side of the grass."

"We're a bunch of misfit people who never belonged any other place."

"We really are at the end of the world."

"We're 125 miles from the city, but they're 212 miles from here."

 ## Denominational Comments

"Conference has become more of a friend rather than just a body."

"Our gradual lack of interest and disconnect from the conference is an issue, although there is a warm feeling that we get knowing that we're connected."

"The conference is what we do together; we work together; and this is an extension of the congregation."

"We're so fortunate to have you here; no, we deserve to have you here."

"I can relate to you because you're honest."

"The pressure to change to resourcing congregations from doing things together comes from the secular and fundamentalist world. We shouldn't go there."

"I want to protect this congregation from the denomination, and at the same time I want to contribute with integrity to the denomination."

"We will go to any place that is providing excellence. We will not allow our denominational membership to keep us from that."

"We don't want membership in the broader church to be 'energy leaks' for us."

"We're a strong conference church."

"Very intrigued by some of the hiring you've done."

"I love this denomination. Where else can you spend three hours in pyjamas with your conference minister?"

"I don't have time to go to the conference. My sock drawer demands too much of my attention."

"How do we do what we really want to do and still remain a good congregation in the broader church?"

"We have not been devout members of MC Canada. You better have better members out there than us."

"We're kind of like an anchor; we drag you down. We simply can't think of a good reason why we should be enthused about being part of MC Canada."

"Is MC Canada relevant at all? Why?"

"The question about what the conference can do for the congregations should be a foreign concept."

"The selling points of a national church body aren't being sold."

"The maximum contribution the conference can make does not meet the minimum needs that we have."

"I'm not a true believer about how our denomination works."

"I'm not sure I want more people to get the *Canadian Mennonite*."

"Your coming here is one of the most visible signs of church leadership that I've seen for a long time."

"We don't get involved in theological controversy. We let the neighbouring church worry about that."

"If you're in business long enough, you're going to be sued."

 *Essence and Identity*

"I love being here. There are so many gifted people here in this church, it's hard to grasp."

"In our congregation there has been a lot of healing that has happened, all of it closely linked to the study of Scripture and its application."

"The Anabaptist vision is getting world-renown recognition, and we're going to be ashamed of it at home? No way!"

"Our greatest strength could also be our greatest weakness. Newcomers could mess up our community."

"'Seed-sowing ministry' is our euphemism for love us and leave us."

"We are the church to the strong and the healthy and the converted."

"We need to be happy with who we are and not try to be someone we're not."

"The basic attitude in the Mennonite constituency in terms of homosexuality is irrelevant to the needs of our society."

"I could care less how they are in other churches; we don't have to worry about following someone else's guidelines."

"When we left the previous church, we wanted to use the German language for ten more years, and now it's already been forty-three years."

"The only thing ever written in stone were the Ten Commandments, so we should be free to strike out on our own."

"We need to sit at the feet of Jesus and not worry so much about activism. But it made it difficult to preach on the book of James. It felt like I had to get a whip and thrash the dear sheep."

"Some people view Jesus as a 'forgiveness' token that can be cashed in for salvation at the end. Mennonites see salvation as integrated into all of life and informs how we live daily. That is quite different."

"Our struggle is to become real Anabaptists, even though we are among Mennonites."

"How do we connect with how God's Spirit is at work in the lives of people who come? We have a gay couple who find this a welcoming place."

"Mennonite people are a communal people."

"Mennonite means the love of God in action."

"What we feed ourselves is what we get."

"Does God's Word change in thirty years? I hope not."

"We try to be more self-sufficient and don't draw on conferences resources very much."

"There are all kinds of churches around here and they are all good, but we've got the best answers."

"I hope as a congregation we don't think we have all the answers but hope that God's word doesn't change."

"I have some absolute beliefs and I'm sorry I can't back down from them. That doesn't mean I won't talk to you."

"Some of the issues that challenge us are whether women should be allowed to cut their hair: this is very strong; and the head covering: we are doing various things in this; divorce and remarriage: we know where we stand; and the homosexuality issue: we're watching and it wouldn't be hard for us to walk away if it goes the wrong way."

"Believing and following is not connected for many."

"Mennonite identity was so deeply rooted in our congregation that it was assumed."

"We've tried to be a 'Mennonite in brackets' kind of congregation. And that doesn't work."

"If the Anglican Book of Common Prayer was good enough for Paul and Silas, it's good enough for us."

"There's not too much to learn here about how to handle the sexuality issue."

"We've been silenced. And it's hard to learn to be quiet over and over."

"You simply do not dismiss family. That's not how it works."

"Our congregation is now large enough to have the poles."

"Twenty years ago we made the decision to stop using conference Sunday school material, and started using David Cook instead. Since then we've 'won' some people, but we've 'lost' our peoplehood."

"I would hate to see our church become a statistic in the chew-up and spit-out Mennonite world."

"At our very worst, we're like a Christian country club where God is just one more member."

"We kind of like get in a rut and we kind of like to stay there."

"Our church is the only one that is not political."

"Mennonite church is the 'first alternative' for a lot of people here."

"We are our own worst enemies by making cultural things Mennonite."

"There is inherited power within the church, and as long as it is benevolent it is no problem."

"I don't want to do the 'Mennonite thing' anymore, so I'll go to Eden Tabernacle; and then I realized that this is doing the 'Mennonite thing.'"

"The executive leadership in the denomination is in a tough spot. The obvious need is to come out and lead the church toward the acceptance of gay/lesbian marriages. But being 'chicken-shit,' leadership is always concerned about division and conflict."

"Our church is a hiding place for Mennonites who want to get away from their churches."

"I'm over-discerned."

"People are more excited about this congregation than they are about God."

"We have an impoverished vocabulary of faith here."

"I am denominationally agnostic."

"We are reminded that special memories are built even as we live this day."

"We are an inclusive church. That is basic. That's who we are. That's how we do church."

"We like our summers off from church."

"We are discouraged but very hopeful."

"We want to set this church on fire."

"We have a low-profile, hidden church kind of concept."

"God has dealt us a very good hand. We need to play our cards carefully."

 *Intergenerational Dynamics/Youth and Young Adults*

"I believe the older people are happy we're here, but they just don't know how to show it yet."

"If it's true that the CEO has to sign on to needed change for it to be successful, in our congregation the CEO is the seniors group. Nothing much can happen here unless they sign on."

"We weep when we see how precious the children are, and we don't want to cause them to stumble."

"Churches that are paying attention to kids and youth are churches that are growing."

"The power of children to draw in their parents is what we're seeing here."

"It's neat being part of a small church where kids have peers."

"The children's story here is like the resurrection. One toot and everyone scoots. It's a real sign of new life, of new energy, and new possibility."

"Children in the past have often been the hidden people, and we're improving in that."

"If I'm with a young person then I'm young, and when I'm with an older person then I'm old."

"We have lots of young couples but we have few babies, and so we need to preach more on the first part of Genesis in the next while."

"Seems like every age group feels left out."

"We are a group of old elders."

"Our senior population is declining. I only have to count one on the back bench."

"They have taken us under their wing and look after us."

"I am so proud of those little shitters."

"What's energizing about this congregation is that young people come and they fall in love with us. Also we discover them."

"It's tough to be a youthful Christian in this culture."

"Grandma, why don't you come to my church; the people in your church are all old."

"We have to fight for the front seats because the youth are always there."

 *Leadership Development*

"If we're not part of the solution, we're part of the problem. So what are we doing about calling and forming leaders?"

"All the stuff I've learned I've learned through MC Canada."

"We've never had power struggles. Our elders have never resisted handing over power."

"As long as anyone wants to chair, they are welcome to do so for as long as they want."

"There are a large number of leaders who don't know our 'soul' and come from traditions that have a strong centralized authority."

"The challenge for leadership will be to get us old fogies off our butts to do something."

"I like making friends with pastors, because the Bible tells me that when I give them a cup of water I'll receive the same reward they get."

"It seems so strange and foreign to us to think that we might be in a position to teach anyone else anything about leadership or about a faith issue."

"Very seldom do you see a player go out at the top. But that's the way it is happening here with our pastor. There is such genuine love here for our pastor."

"We bring the lamb to slaughter [pastoral evaluation] and ask whether we'll swing the axe or not."

"One of my survival techniques is to have call-display at home."

"What we need to learn is how to engage the passion that people exhibit."

"We need to raise up leaders who will move the church beyond the church."

"I hear people say that the people outside the church aren't paying the salaries of the pastors."

"Spiritual disciplines are not spiritual caffeine to help us keep pace with our society."

"I just been elected to lead a conference that doesn't know if it wants to be led."

##  Mission: Local and Global

"The church is only as strong as the people it sends out."

"I'm almost excited about the crisis; there is a nugget of opportunity here."

"As we feel better about ourselves, we're no longer afraid to invite others."

"Why have we grown? We understand what we believe, embrace it, and then push our limits."

"It's at times when we're vulnerable that God's Spirit can most affect us."

"God used the hard times to make us more mature."

"Our church had outreach this year: this Christmas we sang the *Friedensfurst* in English."

"We are getting mixed messages that maybe our concerns about ministry are more about our guilt than about the welfare of the community."

"Our church is an island; we have absolutely nothing to do with our geographic environment."

"We are well adjusted to our society in general but totally disconnected to our community."

##  Missional Church Impact

"There is such a spirit of joy and warm friendships in this congregation."

"People just want to stay; we can't get them to leave."

"I give thanks for the dairy farm and the church. It's easy to work in a place you love."

"Telling and retelling stories of grace we have experienced creates a culture of grace in our congregation."

"We attract people with people, not with programs."

"Our congregation is like a beautiful songbird. We are small, but we have everything we need to be who we are."

"Are you a church or are you a mission? We are a mission."

"Why are people wanting to get baptized? Because they want to be part of a missional church."

"The more you practice love, the more love you get; some come to church for what they can give; others for what they can get."

"We don't want to be welcomed; we want to be embraced. And there is a big difference."

"It's easy to welcome people; to embrace them is challenging."

"We have a basic policy: we want to have our doors open and this means that we must have open hearts."

"Visitation is the blood of pastoring."

"God works in ways we don't even think and know about."

"We have a good heartbeat; we're breathing well; yet there are things we need to work at."

"People have embraced new people and walked with them through difficult stuff. We do know how to adapt."

"We'd like to be a loving community, but at this point we could only say that we are a caring community."

"It would be great to work with black and whites, but that's not the world we live in."

"I can't give you a specific answer, but I can give you a sense of hope."

"Whatever we are doing in our lives is ministry for God."

"We're not playing games here; we're very deep here."

"It's amazing how God's church in the community is working together."

"Forgiveness doesn't mean one side is right; it means that there is a channel through which love can flow."

"Is our experience transferable to others? Amen, it's the kingdom; for sure, it's transferable."

"We don't just want to bring them into religion but into relationship with the Lord."

"We committed spiritual adultery in which the church became more important than the family."

"Our congregation's cup is more than half full; it's running into the saucer by now."

"Welcome to our church; we don't have room for you but welcome anyway."

"We don't want to be an island; we want to be part of the larger church."

"Somehow when we invite God's Spirit to work, it suddenly shows up and surprises us."

"This tastes like more; the missional thinking has started to grab ahold of people."

"God is moving somehow, and basically we just need to take advantage of it."

"Missional peace theology is great."

"The word *missional* confused us all; now we're recognizing across the street and forgot about around the world."

"People have come from discouragement into encouragement, and that's exciting."

"Dialogue must contain the possibility of transformation."

"This is a safe place to bring your problems. And there are not a lot of places like that."

"Relationship is building a bridge that's strong enough to carry the truth."

"We need to trust that at the heart of who we are we will be attractive."

"Ministry becomes a real avenue for creativity."

"Our congregation is ecologically friendly. We could disappear without a trace. And no one would realize that we've been here nor that we've left."

"If you pray for people and make yourself available, God seems to find you."

"If you will become a member, you have to put your shoulder to the wheel."

 ## *Polity, Authority, and Decision Making*

"Change just kind of happens around here. I don't announce too many goals. I just implement them."

"We just make changes without telling anyone that's what we're doing."

"We don't want to get into the habit of using our few resources only for ourselves, but to share what we have with others."

"What is important is not what we retain, but what we can share."

"I don't run the church; I just make sure it gets run."

"We decide to deal with issues before there are issues. We try to do that as a congregation. No issue, no names."

"We allow people to vote yes with a heavy heart. And that has been helpful."

"We're comfortable with the tension of the grey."

"We should have enough confidence in our leadership who know where we come from and where we're going."

"If you work on something long enough, you can get it in the back door."

"When a new pastor comes, we'll be back to see what happens."

"If in doubt, we do nothing."

"There's no room for dictatorship around here."

"It's ownership; it's our church—at least the ones who stayed."

"Our church is okay. No one yells at membership meetings anymore."

"It's been many years since we've voted on something in our congregation. If we can't come to consensus, we haven't done it."

"Walking into the church used to be like walking into a chicken barn and yelling boo; all the leg-horn hens were along the back wall."

"Basically, the key is to always have people think they are the front row in decision making."

"We're great at sugar coating issues, and then we pussyfoot around."

 *Priorities and Strategies*

"When you have a head of the family, it draws you together; and when you lose that, you sort of drift."

"When our pastors left, we were like on a boat that was sinking."

"Our pastor sees the forest but also sees every individual tree."

"At our annual meeting, I can holler at people and everyone takes it very well."

"We haven't had an election in church for a long time. Everybody just gets appointed."

"How we get there is important."

"You get out what you put into it."

"Northern Ontario is a raw material location."

"The ship (church building) is built; now we need to sail it."

"There is no one here that is pressured to stop doing what they are doing."

"Past experience has taught us that we can't know the future."

"For us men, if there's not a woman around, we don't meet."

"Some congregations have the sense of sleep-walking, but there is death here."

"'Congregation is everything' seems to be the motto we are moving toward."

"We stopped meeting in small groups because not everyone could be included."

 ## Structuring for Effectiveness

"We have a budgeting rule: 50 percent of our donations must go beyond the congregation. This has encouraged giving. We have no trouble meeting our budget. Our budget has almost doubled in the last eight years."

"We're on board, but we still like to keep a stick in the spokes."

"Church membership is a tough concept to sell here."

"Just like the eagle kicks the young out of the nest, this is what happened to us; we now take steps for change willingly."

"We've always been a loving church. We've made course corrections, but we've not been entirely reborn."

"People that do come are fairly broken, and we need to flex and adapt very quickly now."

"People are the permanent pastoral presence in the church and work with the pastor who is less permanent."

"Don't take a position in the church because you should but because you want to."

"We are open to change a little bit."

"How to make horizontal relationship in a hierarchical culture—that's our challenge."

"When you get more people to invest, they care more."

"Our congregation appears to be developmentally stuck."

"We've never not met our commitments to the broader church."

"For many years the word *budget* was verboten [forbidden] in our congregation."

"If we need money, somehow it's just there."

"This has been an amazingly gracious congregation to pastoral leadership."

"We are a congregation, not a parish."

"We just got tired of hearing about the Ladies Salad Supper, so we organized the Men's Meat Meal. And that's been very successful."

 **Tour Comments**

"What we are doing here today is absolutely essential."

"Your visit here feels very generous."

"This church made your radar screen, and it matters. What a gift that is to us."

"Thanks for these four questions. They are right on. If we would have done a think tank in our own congregation, these are the questions we should have asked."

"It's a world of difference that you have come to visit rather than waiting for us to come to you. Thank you so much for coming."

"Our council said that for you to come to visit us is a tremendous signal of servant leadership, and we appreciate that very much."

"The guys at the coffee shop send their greetings to you."

"Thank you for taking seriously our separate identity and coming directly to us instead of treating us as a cluster. This is important to us. You have treated us as someone and not just as a source of donations."

"Your visit shows that the whole church cares for each individual congregation."

"It is so significant that when the general secretary takes the time to listen and visit, this is a real service."

"I think your visit has changed my perspective. If you can go to all the time and trouble to come and see us here in this little place, maybe I need to make more of an effort to go to the assembly and also see what's going on beyond us here. I will reconsider coming to assembly this year."

 ### *Unity and Diversity*

"I don't have any enemies in the congregation."

"Our former interim pastor contributed greatly by running a harrow over the field. He detonated every land mine that was in the congregation."

"Ten years ago we were like a couple of German shepherds first meeting each other, circling each other from a distance and snarling at each other."

"We've now developed an atmosphere in which folks are praying for the congregation instead of against it."

"Our biggest asset is our sense of community. But sometimes we don't want that sense disturbed."

"We've had one family in the last twenty years that left because of frustration. There is a strong church family."

"Other churches have never attracted our people. It doesn't make any sense to leave."

"We've been through adversity, but we really have only lost two people."

"Our advice is that when you come together, eat first, and then you don't have as many tensions."

"We always have a choice. We can choose to allow things to divide or unite us."

"The biggest bone of contention in the congregation is where we will have our annual campout."

"We're a small congregation; we can't afford to have conflict."

"The problem is that we haven't been listening to our own church."

"I'm a new Christian, and it was just the natural thing to keep coming here to church. So I prayed that if there was anything missing here I wanted to be a part of supplying it."

"How can we find common ground with Asian kids, Hispanic kids, East Indian kids, and English kids all in one room?"

"How much do we really know each other? In other words, would we shed tears for them at their funerals?"

"Sometimes the same thing that unites us is what can also divide us, for example, food and the *Confession of Faith*."

"We are committed to unity."

"Every time someone leaves, part of our heart goes with them."

"No. Homosexuality is an issue we cannot answer because then we would have another bunch of persons leaving."

"Our philosophy is to talk first and fight later."

"If we don't find a solution on the first day, then we take another day, no problem. It's important to be communal."

"Sharing time in worship is when the community keeps itself honest."

"Sharing time in worship is a big leveller; it brings together the extremes and forces each one to deal with the other. It's a discipline that helps us listen to each other."

"We understand that if there's conflict in the church, that's a terrible witness."

"We deliberately try to respect other viewpoints."

"We don't try to argue with people, but let them go."

"We need to learn to love people we don't like."

"It's one thing to say we are a community; it's another to be a community."

"They're wired differently than we are."

"This is meant to be a French-English expression of the body of Christ."

"This church has taken in people from so many different backgrounds and mixed them up, and it works and it's great."

"We don't really plan much into the future. There is enough evil to deal with one day at a time."

"What irritates me is the idea that if we don't agree with someone, we don't accept them."

"Some are saying we are too liberal and others that we are stuck in the mud."

"Some in our congregation are stepping on the gas and some are stepping on the brake, and a vehicle needs both to function properly."

"I'm not sure that breaking the barriers is the right word, but maybe penetrating them a little bit."

"New people that are coming have a bit of a faith background and are not 'raw pagans' off the street."

"Drawing lines in the sand never takes us anywhere."

"By continuing discussion for some closes the discussion."

"I can see the world very differently than someone else, but that doesn't mean that I'll take my ball and play in a different court."

"It's best to be silent because the divisions are so deep."

"We have synergy on the church benches."

"It's okay if we're not cookie cutter; it's okay to be different."

"Are we an endangered species if we get along with each other?"

"We know that everybody has quills. If we don't like each other, you tolerate each other. If you're not my best friend, you're still my friend."

"We are at peace—maybe too much; there are no clouds in the sky for us."

"As long as we stay away from some topics like politics and theology, we get along okay."

"It would never occur to me that I don't like someone."

"I'm not sure we like each other, but we do care for each other."

"There's no one in this room I don't like."

"I remember that congregational meetings once were difficult, and now I like everyone here. It takes the life right out of the meetings."

"Why not be united, because we do a lot of committee work here."

"We don't have a huge ship that we can afford a lot of spill."

"The people who gave me the worst phone calls have now become my best friends."

"So far our strengths are stronger than our tensions."

"If there are no problems, we're not alive."

"We've had two battles and one skirmish in our history as a congregation."

"We are an immigrant church with an unnatural composition of membership."

"We like each other a lot; there's a lot of love here; I can't remember when I was mad last."

"It's hard to explain how close we feel to each other."

"I'd rather be part of the solution rather than trying to avoid things."

"The people we attract will not be the well-behaved Christians. How do you give them something meaningful to do?"

"We're a Mennonite church partnering with an Anglican church to do a Baptist vacation Bible school."

"Nobody that I know of has left the community."

"We don't have any bruises to show for our infighting."

"The most important ingredients here are love and respect for one another."

"The struggles of the past have drawn people closer together; we need each other."

"We rarely meet as a group without a potluck. And this shows."

"We reserve the freedom to say what we think and feel, and we often laugh. There have been enough tears. This softens our communications."

"We've realized that we just can't go it alone. We realize that we need others."

"Maybe we have forgotten to listen to the other one."

"How can we study something that people fear so much?"

"My wound is not as deep as a well and not as wide as a church door" (Shakespeare).

"For a little while, if the pain is too great, it's important to step off the tack."

"In our congregation, people don't need to turn off their minds at the door. We are a welcoming church without being a 'welcoming church.'"

"We'll get through the issues we're facing."

"How can you help us? Create an issue in the church that isn't homosexuality."

"First the government creates poverty and then they sell the food."

*Volunteerism*

"We have very willing horses sharing the load."

"There is no fatigue in our church that is dragging us down; there is buoyancy that is helping us a lot."

"We're good at passing the buck."

 *Worship and Music*

"We do not tolerate the question, 'what do I like in a worship service?' But rather 'what enables us to worship well?' That's the question we need to answer."

"You don't worship if you hate to go to church, and therefore sometimes the life of congregations don't facilitate the possibility of worship."

"Music keeps me sane; I sing to the cows."

"We're singing 'songs' now instead of choruses and hymns."

"If we weren't real wise people who love each other, we would have conflict about worship."

"The drummer is one of our members, so we have to tolerate him."

"We just got the new blue hymnals. Well, they're not new for others, but they are new for us."

"You have to decide what matters more—the people or the music."

"I can't even make a joyful noise to the Lord."

"In our congregation we don't need to say, 'I crashed my car this week, praise the Lord.'"

"Let's define this sexuality thing. I want them to avoid twenty-five years of hell on earth."

"This is our identity, and if we don't do something with it, no one else will."

"Our service at this point doesn't reflect who we are but who we will become."

# Notes

1. "Paul sees these assemblies as communities of salvation. . . . They are participating in the divine craziness that transformed the suffering of Jesus into the means of reconciling a hostile world (1 Corinthians 1:18-31)." (Tom Yoder Neufeld, "Are you saved?" *Vision* 7:1 (Spring 2007), 8.)

2. It is important to define *church* a bit more carefully here. I am using this word in the sense of the New Testament *ek-klesia*. This Greek word combines two parts. The *klesia* is related to the verb form *kaleo* and the noun form *klesis*, which means a calling (to call) or a vocation. So at the very root of our understanding of the church there needs to be a commitment to its vocation/calling: "to lead a life worthy of the *calling* to which you have been *called*" (Ephesians 4:1, emphasis added). The word itself resists being defined firstly in terms of structure, organization, institution, program, buildings, or bureaucracy. In other words, the very assumptions we often make when talking about "church" are not what the root of this word would point to. "Church" is a people with a vocation (or a vocationed people); it is a calling to walk worthily in particular ways. It is an "assembly of vocation." The "vocation" (*klesis*), in turn, is defined by the light shed on God's will and way through the experience with Jesus of Nazareth. How God's reign looks and how it comes has been redefined, or at least paradigmatically clarified, via God's revelation through the experience of Christ. This is what makes the church "Christian."

The second part of the word *ek-klesia* is the prefix *ek*. Literally this means "out of." The possibilities of meaning are multiple when linked to its root *klesis*. It likely refers to a "vocation" that is separate, different, away from, or called out from other "vocations." It also refers to the assembly of persons who respond to that separate vocation. It should not be read to mean that the vocation itself is "separate" from the context or the world in which the assembly is found. Indeed the vision for the *ekklesia* in the rest of the letter would militate against such an understanding. The "vocationed peoplehood" is not "called out" in order to disconnect from the world, but is "called out" to connect to the world in a different way, a way that would put

Jesus at the centre of understanding God's will and way for God's reign to be inaugurated and for restoration and reconciliation to become real. When the vocation becomes communal, it becomes the church.

# The Author

Robert J. Suderman became general secretary of Mennonite Church Canada in December 2005 after serving as executive secretary of Mennonite Church Canada Witness since 2000. From 1968 to 1985, he taught at schools and colleges in Canada and Bolivia. He was a founding director of CLARA, the Latin American Anabaptist Resource Center in Colombia, and of Mennonite Biblical Seminary of Colombia, where he served from 1989 to 1994. Suderman was born in Winkler, Manitoba.

"Robert J. Suderman opens a window into the heart and soul of a denomination, and of a people. By taking seriously the 'wisdom from the pews' we see through the programs and ministries of this denomination and right into her hopes and dreams, her pain and anguish, and her place in Canadian culture today. Suderman brilliantly extracts and articulates trends and issues of the church from his 230 congregational visits and roots them in a compelling vision for the future."
—Janet Plenert, Executive Secretary of Mennonite Church Canada Witness

"In *God's People Now!* Robert J. Suderman offers a unique and inviting window into the identity, life, concerns, and aspirations of a denomination with a rich history and significant presence in Canada. We are invited to listen in on conversations with its members and consider the reflections of a leader of a community of faith seeking to be a faithful witness in twenty-first century Canada."
—Bruce J. Clemenger, President of Evangelical Fellowship of Canada

"Robert J. Suderman has taken on an ambitious task; but not a task, a ministry—to hear what the congregations of the Mennonite Church Canada were saying and to help them hear each other. His visits and this book dedicate themselves to encouraging goodwill and closer relationships, cooperation and partnerships. It is the calling for all Christians to truly hear ourselves as church and to use that hearing for the glory of God."
—Rev. Dr. Karen Hamilton, General Secretary of the Canadian Council of Churches

"Jack Suderman's unorthodox idea to visit all 230 Mennonite Church Canada churches in under three months turns into a journey that reaches the hearts and souls of congregations. While not minimizing the pain or the challenges they face, this is an uplifting, provocative, poignant, and ultimately hopeful book that re-calls the church to its original mission. Important reading for pastors and for congregations."
—Marianne Mellinger, Mennonite Church Eastern Canada

"By reflecting back what he heard, Jack Suderman helps us appreciate more fully who we are, in all our exhilarating and sometimes exasperating diversity. By helping us reflect on what he heard, Jack helps us envision who we might become—if we allow our spiritual imagination to be unleashed in the church."
—Henry Paetkau, President of Conrad Grebel University College